DEALING WITH Y(

How To Books on business and management

Arranging Insurance
Be a Freelance Sales Agent
Buy & Run a Shop
Buy & Run a Small Hotel
Buying a Personal Computer
Collecting a Debt
Communicate at Work
Conducting Effective Interviews
Conducting Effective Negotiations
Conducting Staff Appraisals
Coping with Self-Assessment
Counsel People at Work
Dealing with Your Bank
Delivering Customer Service
Do Your Own Advertising
Do Your Own PR
Doing Business Abroad
Employ & Manage Staff
Investing in People
Investing in Stocks & Shares
Keep Business Accounts
Manage a Sales Team
Manage an Office
Manage Computers at Work
Manage People at Work
Managing Budgets & Cash Flows
Managing Credit

Managing Meetings
Managing Projects
Managing Yourself
Market Yourself
Master Public Speaking
Mastering Book-Keeping
Mastering Business English
Organising Effective Training
Preparing a Business Plan
Publish a Book
Publish a Newsletter
Raise Business Finance
Sell Your Business
Setting Up Your Own Limited
  Company
Start a Business From Home
Start Your Own Business
Starting to Manage
Successful Mail Order Marketing
Taking on Staff
Understand Finance at Work
Use the Internet
Winning Presentations
Write a Press Release
Write & Sell Computer Software
Writing a Report
Writing Business Letters

Further titles in preparation

The How To Series now contains more than 200 titles in the following categories:

Business Basics
Family Reference
Jobs & Careers
Living & Working Abroad

Mind & Body
Student Handbooks
Successful Writing

Please send for a free copy of the latest catalogue for full details
(see back cover for address).

How To Books

BUSINESS BASICS

DEALING WITH YOUR BANK

How to assert yourself as a paying customer

Brian Cain

How To Books

Cartoons by Mike Flanagan

British Library Cataloguing in Publication Data
A catalogue record for this book is available from the British Library.

© Copyright 1997 by Brian Cain.

First published in 1997 by How To Books Ltd, 3 Newtec Place,
Magdalen Road, Oxford OX4 1RE, United Kingdom.
Tel: (01865) 793806. Fax: (01865) 248780.

Note: The material contained in this book is set out in good faith for
general guidance and no liability can be accepted for loss or expense
incurred as a result of relying in particular circumstances on statements
made in the book. The laws and regulations are complex and liable to
change, and readers should check the current position with the relevant
authorities before making personal arrangements.

Produced for How To Books by Deer Park Productions.
Typeset by PDQ Typesetting, Stoke-on-Trent, Staffs.
Printed and bound by Cromwell Press, Broughton Gifford, Melksham,
Wiltshire.

Contents

List of Illustrations

Preface

Arranging the banking services you need both personally and for any business you are involved with is one of the most important transactions you will enter into during your life. It ranks in importance alongside buying a house or changing jobs. Indeed, the matters discussed in this book are intimately connected to both those events!

The explosion of the financial services market, and the plethora of products offered by banks, building societies, insurance companies, credit card companies and others has created a difficult task for those wishing to buy financial services. They first have to understand the basics, so that they understand the information they pick up along the way to opening accounts and investing in things such as a pension. The aim of this book is to provide readers with the information they will need to sift through the marketing material, understand any jargon and make a reasoned choice when they pay for financial services.

We have all had occasion to question the service which our bank or building society has provided. Whether it is the charges which appear on your statements, or the conditions attached to a particular type of mortgage, the basic points you need to bear in mind when dealing with your bank or complaining about its service can be found in these pages.

Over the course of the average lifetime most people spend thousands, if not tens of thousands of pounds, on investments, bank loans, overdrafts, credit cards, agreements, pensions and advice on financial questions concerning them. This book will help you to spend that money wisely.

Finally, I would like to thank Morag McIvor for her help in preparing this book.

Brian Cain

DO YOU WANT TO?

- Take control of your personal and business finances

- Plan a savings strategy for your future

- Open the right type of savings account

- Know more about mortgages and guarantees

- Negotiate the terms of a personal or business loan

- Make the most effective use of banking services

- Avoid incurring unnecessary costs and charges

- Apply for a credit card

- Learn how to calculate the costs of buying on credit

- Find out more about automatic teller machines and electronic banking

- Assert your rights in any disputes with banks and building societies

- Obtain free advice on debts and escape the debt trap

Is This You?

Bank customer   Borrower

Credit card user

Shopkeeper   Homeowner

Small businessperson

Guarantor   Paid by money transfer

Planning retirement

Company director   Buying on credit

Disputing with a lender

Opening an account   On-line shopper

Instructing financial advisers

Worried about debt   Applying for a loan

Confused about debit cards

Received a demand   Treasurer

Looking for a mortgage

Seeking a new lender   Finance director

Proposing a voluntary arrangement

Student with loan   Working in financial sector

Hate banking jargon

Debt counsellor   Trainee solicitor

Trainee accountant

1
Managing Your Money

BUYING BANKING SERVICES

Paying for service
It is easy to forget that when using a bank, building society or other financial institution you are paying for a service. You may not receive a monthly bill for 'banking services rendered', but for most people there will be a **charge**. A bank may charge you a monthly fee, it will charge interest on sums borrowed or even a daily fee on some overdrafts. It will use your money in its business to create income for itself. *You* are paying any institution which holds your money for the services it provides to you. In exchange for the contribution you make towards that organisation's business, you are entitled to a good quality service.

Shopping around
Making a good 'purchase' in this context involves keeping your money with an organisation which gives you the right type of service:

- in the right place
- for the right price
- delivered in the right manner.

As in buying any other goods or services, it pays to shop around for banking and other financial services. The range of services offered by high street banks and building societies is vast. You are unlikely to find that one organisation gives you the best deal for every type of service you need, from loans to car or contents insurance.

Information equals power – bargaining power.

If you know that Company A provides a travellers' cheques

service with a lower rate of commission than your own bank or building society, you may be able to agree a reduction in your own bank's commission rate. Your bank or building society will know you can go elsewhere and that is a powerful incentive for it to keep you happy by discounting its rates. After all, when you pop into one of its rivals to get your holiday money they may take the opportunity to persuade you to switch your account to them.

ASSESSING YOUR WEALTH

Taking stock

The best banking packages do not come 'off the peg', but are designed for you personally with regard for your individual circumstances. Taking stock of your current position will enable you to make a better informed decision about the type of services you will use and the particular type of **current** or **savings accounts** you may need. It is a good idea to prepare a statement which sets out your existing financial position. Producing a **financial profile** will give you a better idea of:

- what you have (**assets**)
- and what you owe (**liabilities**).

Equally important, it will give you an idea of the manner in which your cash needs fluctuate throughout the year: your **cash flow**. This is important in budgeting for any peaks and troughs in your receipts (money in) and expenses (money out). If your profile shows that you will need more cash than you earn in any particular month, you will know that you have to either arrange an overdraft or call on savings. Forward planning even to this limited extent will save the cost of fees, or protect your entitlement to interest on savings.

Taking advice

Assessing how much you have, and subsequently preparing a personal financial profile, will also help you if you need to obtain advice concerning your finances. Getting advice and entering into agreements to obtain financial services can often be more an act of blind faith than reasoned choice. Taking the time to look at your present financial circumstances is the essential first step on the road to complete confidence in managing your finances in the future.

PREPARING A PERSONAL FINANCIAL PROFILE

Identifying income and expenditure
Your financial profile should distinguish between:

- assets which may be sold for cash relatively quickly (**liquid** or **realisable assets**)

- assets which ordinarily you would not sell or would require some time to do so (**illiquid** or **long-term assets**), such as any value or **equity** in your home if you are a home owner.

Just as there are long- and short-term assets, there are short-term liabilities which have to be paid on a regular basis – such as electricity, gas and telephone bills – and long-term liabilities such as annual insurance premiums or tax assessments if you are self-employed. Your financial profile should identify these and allow you to budget for them in good time.

> **Be realistic in estimating the amounts to include in your profile.**

A typical financial profile should show you your:

- monthly income
- monthly expenditure
- disposable income each month
- total annual income
- total annual expenditure
- disposable income each year
- peaks and troughs in receipts and expenditure and when these are likely to occur.

Using financial profiles
Profiles are simply a tool to be used in financial planning. Once calculated, the figures should only be used as guides. Your financial profile should contain a small contingency fund to provide for unexpected liabilities.

A typical profile would look like the one in Figure 1. You may wish to adapt this form to suit your own changing needs. In the meantime you can use it as a template to get you started. You may want to photocopy the form while it is blank for use in the future.

MONTHLY PERSONAL FINANCIAL PROFILE

£

Receipts

Earnings ....

Pension income ....

Interest received ....

Dividends received ....

State benefits ....

Bonus ....

Other (eg expenses repaid, tax repayments) ....

Total monthly receipts _____

Expenses

Home

Mortgage/rent ....

Council tax ....

Utilities

  – telephone ....

  – gas ....

  – water ....

  – electric ....

  – TV licence ....

Equipment rental (eg TV, video) ....

Travelling

Fares ....

Car insurance ....

Petrol ....

Repairs ....

Shopping

Food ....

Clothes ....

Borrowings

Loan payments ....

Credit card payments ....

Hire purchase payments ....

Other

Entertainment ....

Newspapers/magazines ....

Contingency fund ....

Total monthly expenses _____

Disposable income = total monthly receipts _____

less **total monthly expenses** _____

Fig. 1. A typical financial profile.

FINANCIAL CALENDAR

Month	Amount (£)	Action required
January		Arrange temporary overdraft to fund car repairs next month
February	1,500	
March		Give notice on 90-day interest account to withdraw £850 to pay for family holiday in June
April		
May		
June	850	
July		
August		
September		
October		
November		
December		

Examples

Two examples have been completed to show you how the financial calendar should work. You could also use it for other reminders you may need in order to organise your finances. For example, you may want to put a note in for March reminding you to top up payments into any pension fund before the end of the tax year on 5 April.

ANNUAL FINANCIAL PROFILE

£

Asset values
  Home ....
  Investments/savings ....
  Cash on deposit ....
  Car ....
  Valuables ....

  Total assets _____

Liabilities
  Mortgage ....
  Loans outstanding ....
  Hire purchase outstanding ....
  Credit cards ....
  Annual payments
    − tax ....
    − holiday ....
    − premiums ....
    − other (eg club memberships, etc)
  Total liabilities _____
  Net assets/liabilities = total assets *less*
  total liabilities _____

Income and expenses

Using disposable income

Monthly **disposable income** is how much 'spare' cash you have each month after essential payments have been made. If you know it is unlikely to be needed in the immediate future, it should be earning interest for you. Some of this sum may be worth putting in an account which limits your access to it but gives you a higher rate of interest. Some of it may be used to top up pension plans or otherwise turned into a longer-term form of investment. The important point is that the profile allows you to see at a glance what you are likely to have available to use in different forms of savings accounts or other investments; these will be covered in succeeding chapters.

Of course, you may find that your profile shows you have no disposable income, that your expenses exceed your income over a month. In this case you need to plan for borrowings, after assessing whether you can properly afford the costs involved in borrowing, or reduce your outgoings. These subjects are also covered later, as is the difficult question of escaping the debt trap and where you may obtain help if you are finding it hard to cope.

Using net assets

If you have **net assets**, that is, the final figure on the annual financial profile is positive, you have to decide whether that asset can be made to work for you more effectively. Can you turn that asset into an investment which would provide more value to you than simply leaving it alone? If the figure is positive because the value of your house has increased over time, you may want to leave it alone. There are schemes to release this value (also referred to as the equity in your house), but they are relatively complicated and require specialist advisers. If your asset is largely made up of cash on deposit, you could open a **TESSA** account which offers tax-free returns (see page 85), or buy **with-profits insurance**, **unit trust** or other investments.

Making the most of your money is a job in itself. The amount you receive for doing this usually depends on the effort you put into managing your finances.

Ideas for different types of investment and saving appear throughout the book.

Dealing with debt

If the figure for disposable income and net assets is negative, this means that your liabilities exceed your assets and you need to look closely at changing the way your finances are organised. This is dealt with in Chapter 9. There is no need to panic. Think about the following:

* Is there a source of income you have overlooked, for instance are you now entitled to some state benefit or a tax repayment?

* Can you reduce your outgoings?

* Is your disposable income likely to increase in the near future?

* Where can you get some free advice? (See Useful Addresses.)

If you are in financial difficulties, you do not need to sit and wait for creditors to come knocking at your door. Indeed, they will not do so – it is illegal for creditors to harass you. There are many different ways of settling creditors' claims which allow you to start again. You only need to be honest with creditors and with yourself. If you do that, the law is on your side.

Setting objectives

Once you have completed your financial profile, think about why you would like to save. Reasons may include:

* taking a holiday
* buying a new car, computer or clothes
* establishing an emergency fund to help with any future crisis
* putting down a deposit on a house
* weddings
* retirement funds
* home improvements.

If, say, you want to take a holiday in six months' time, instead of leaving your money in a current account you could save it in an account which gives you a higher rate of interest in return for your agreement to give one to three months' notice of withdrawal. If you are planning for retirement, you may want to maximise returns by putting your money into some of the longer-term investments discussed in Chapter 7. The reasons you are saving, and the time by which you hope to achieve your objective, will give you a good idea of the type of account you want to open. This is discussed in the next chapter.

CHOOSING WHERE TO KEEP YOUR MONEY

The last few years have seen some fundamental changes in the banking services industry. You have a much greater choice about where you put your money than ever before. Organisations can now offer a much wider selection of financial services to the public. The advantage is that you have a greater range of products to choose from. The disadvantage is that the availability of so many products can make the task of sifting through advertising material daunting. As with any other service industry, selling techniques differ between organisations. The basic rule is not to allow yourself to be hurried into entering into agreements involving your money. Allow yourself time for reflection on:

- the services offered
- the costs of using these services
- the manner in which they are provided to you.

Most people will want to have an account into which their wages or benefits may be paid or through which cheques can be cleared. These accounts are now available from:

- banks
- building societies
- post offices
- some credit card companies
- some retail stores.

Using banks and building societies
For purely personal banking arrangements there is little to choose between banks and building societies. In general terms banks offer a greater range of accounts, with fewer restrictions, than building societies. Both types of organisation offer interest-bearing current accounts, with cheque books, **automatic teller machine** cards (**ATM** or cash cards) and associated **credit cards**.

Deciding between banks and building societies
In recent years several large building societies have changed their

status to become banks. The commercial reasons for this differ in each case, but the conversion to banks does enable them to provide a wider range of services to customers. As building societies they could not offer some services to customers because of technical restrictions imposed by the legislation which governs the conduct of building societies.

If you are attracted by certain aspects of the services offered by building societies, whether higher interest rates or simply the staff who provide the service, make sure before you open an account that you will be able to obtain any other services you think you may need, easily and without incurring additional costs. For example, some organisations may not be keen to offer business loans to customers who maintain personal accounts elsewhere. Charges for these and other services may be increased if an account is not held with the organisation concerned.

Banking at the post office
There are now two types of account you can hold which are operated through the network of post offices which cover the country.

National savings
National savings has a variety of products available, ranging from children's bonds through ordinary accounts to pensioner bonds. (More about **bonds** as a form of saving in Chapter 7.) National Savings has in excess of 30 million customers. It trades heavily on the fact that, as it is backed by HM Treasury, its customers are the only ones whose money is effectively guaranteed by the government. If you are looking for a 'no frills' banking service, or if you do not pay tax, its products are certainly worth investigating. It does not issue cheque books or ATM cards with ordinary or investment accounts. Additionally, no overdrafts are available to customers of National Savings. If you need cheque books, cash cards and overdraft services you may want to take a look at the other types of account sold through post offices.

Alliance & Leicester Giro
The Alliance & Leicester provides the Alliance & Leicester Giro line of banking services through the post office network, having bought what used to be known as National Giro Bank a few years ago. These accounts offer the usual collection of cheque books, cards, telephone banking and other services, and the convenience of

deposit and withdrawal services at post offices. Although sold through post offices, unlike National Savings, the Alliance & Leicester Giro products are not backed by HM Treasury but by the bank itself.

Saving with credit card companies
Credit card companies sometimes offer interest-bearing accounts to their customers, which give you interest on money in these accounts. Bear in mind that you may need more than just a place to keep your money and consider whether such a company would be best placed to provide any additional services.

Banking with retail stores
Recently more retailers have begun to offer customers bank accounts. Major supermarket chains such as Tesco and Sainsbury's have led the way in this. Find out whether the banking element of any service is actually in association with some other organisation and, if so, whether it would be better to go to that organisation direct. Some of these accounts pay interest on any credit balance (that is, money in the account) and if you are simply looking for an account to earn interest for short periods they are worth considering.

Such retailers often have customer reward schemes, which enhance the benefits of opening such accounts. The range of financial services offered by some of the larger retail stores is growing and they look set to become an important part of the financial services industry.

DECIDING WHAT SERVICES YOU WANT

The following factors may influence your decision on whether to become a customer of a particular organisation.

Branch networks
Establish whether you can withdraw money without a special arrangement at all branches of the organisation.

- Are there any limits on the amount you may withdraw on any one day?

- Is it possible to make special arrangements to make withdrawals at other branches of the organisation and is a fee charged for this? Some companies will view this as an 'extra' service.

With some of the smaller banks and building societies the network of branches may be less extensive than you think. Many building societies operate only in certain regions; you need to discover how you will gain access to your account if you are travelling outside that area.

Automatic teller machines

Automatic teller machines (ATMs) allow access to funds outside normal business hours. You need to ask:

- How extensive is the ATM network?

- Will the ATM card which is issued to you work in machines overseas, so that you can use it on business or holiday trips? Most cash card issuers have links with systems in other countries; their cards carry logos to identify which machines can be used.

- Does the service at an ATM allow you simply to draw out cash and obtain mini statements, or can you also make deposits or even pay bills from those machines?

ATM charges
There will often be a charge if you use one card issuer's ATM card in another organisation's cash machine. This may be either a flat fee of £1 or so, or a small percentage of the amount withdrawn, say 1.5 per cent. If you use the card often, but not at a branch of your bank or building society, these amounts slowly dripping out of your account can make operating it an expensive business.

Debit and credit cards

The card which allows you access to ATMs may also allow you to pay for goods and services by what is known as **electronic funds transfer at point of sale**, sometimes referred to by the acronym **EFTPOS**. Such cards carry logos, Switch and Delta being the most popular, which retailers display to indicate they accept payment by that method. These cards are simply ways of making payments from your account without using cash or having to write a cheque. Making a payment in this manner is discussed in more detail in Chapter 5. Find out at the outset how your organisation's scheme works and how many retailers use that system.

Differences between debit and credit cards
A **debit card** differs from a credit card in a number of important ways, which are discussed in Chapter 4. Some debit cards carry a

Visa logo. Visa is also a major credit card issuer. Be careful about the terms of use which attach to your particular card, as buying with a credit card may give you valuable rights against the card issuer which you will not obtain if you use a debit card.

Loans

Initially you may not want to borrow money. The chances are, however, that at some stage you will need to borrow and it pays to find out what services are on offer when opening an account. It is at this stage, when the bank or building society is keen to obtain your custom, that they may be most willing to give you the best terms for a loan or overdraft, or cut fees on some other service.

Loans range from a simple **overdraft** to a **term loan** which may be for either personal or business use. Not all financial organisations can offer business loans. Different types of loans, and an explanation of how to apply for one, are described in Chapter 3.

Telephone banking

Telephone banking allows you to carry out transactions on your account, confirm your balance, apply for loans and pay bills from the comfort of your own home, office or nearest telephone box. Most banks offer this service at no extra cost to customers, although the hours during which the service is available differ from one organisation to the next. Some are available twenty-four hours a day, 365 days a year, others only until 8 pm during weekdays and not at all at weekends.

Other products

The other services which are offered by an organisation may be an important factor in making your choice. If you are a parent, the availability of children's accounts at your own branch may be important. Students will be looking for special deals on loans and insurances. From time to time you may need services such as foreign exchange for holidays or business trips, advice on investments, insurance advice, somewhere to store valuables or help with wills and probate. Finally, ask about services which the organisation hopes to provide in the future, such as **smartcards** which are likely to become as widely used as cash cards are now. These are described in Chapter 5.

FINDING THE BEST DEAL

You can obtain a lot of information about the services on offer from different financial institutions by:

- Looking at advertisements in the financial sections of newspapers and magazines. The weekend papers are particularly good.

- Asking friends and family about their experiences with their banks and building societies.

- Taking a walk through the nearest town centre to pick up leaflets in branches of banks, building societies and other financial organisations.

- Telephoning the freephone numbers provided by organisations offering such services.

- Looking at the Teletext pages which contain information about some financial organisations.

- Looking at the pages on the Internet where organisations advertise.

Looking at advertisements

The Advertising Standards Authority
The Advertising Standards Authority states that, in relation to financial services and products, all advertisements should give details of any limitations, expenses, penalties and charges which might affect the contract formed between a bank or building society and its customers. If the advertisement is short or general in content, free explanatory material giving full details of the products on offer should be readily available to the potential customer before any agreement is entered into. When reading any advertisement, it is worth bearing in mind that:

- The small print will usually contain the bad news such as restrictions on access to your money and costs.

- You should always obtain any further details which are available and read them carefully.

- Interest rates will vary over time unless they are 'fixed'.

- Favourite advertising phrases like 'tax free', 'interest paid gross', 'net of tax', all mean something different and will affect the return on your money. (These phrases are discussed in the next chapter.)

Relying on advertisements

Do not rely on an advertisement too heavily. It will only give you a general impression of the service on offer. The contract between you and the bank regulates your rights, and this contract will be governed by detailed terms and conditions which you will receive before opening an account. It is in the detailed terms and conditions that you will find specific statements about restrictions on withdrawal, the availability of overdrafts and any charges which will be imposed.

Misleading advertisements

Financial institutions are well regulated in terms of what should appear in their advertisements. In addition to the general rules which apply to all advertisements, such as being 'fair' and 'readily understandable', banks, building societies and other organisations are governed by special legislation which ensures that they should not mislead potential customers. If you feel you have been misled by an advertisement:

- First try to talk the matter through with someone in authority at the branch. The manager may have discretion to deal with small disputes which arise.

- The local Trading Standards Department may be interested in any advertisements which are misleading. Their telephone enquiry service may be able to suggest solutions.

- Have a talk with someone at the Banking or Building Societies' Ombudsman's office (see page 109).

- Any statements contained in advertisements may be binding on your bank. Consequently the bank may be compelled to act in accordance with the statements made in the advertisements. This is so whether or not the detailed terms and conditions contain statements which conflict with the advertising. It is worth bearing this in mind when writing letters of complaint or, in the last resort, instructing solicitors to help solve the problem.

Making a personal visit

It is always sensible to make a personal visit to the local branch you will be using. This gives you some idea of the quality of service you are likely to receive. A visit made in the lunch hour will also help you assess how quickly you can expect to be served in a busy period.

Ask for an interview with the manager or one of his more senior staff. Although staff may change during your time as a customer, such a chat will enable you to form an opinion on the training of staff and whether it is the right kind of set-up for you. How long it takes to get to see a senior member of staff gives you an idea of how busy these people are. Ask a few questions about the restrictions, costs and rates of interest and see if the responses coincide with the advertising material you have seen. A good financial organisation will have staff who know all the nooks and crannies of their own products. If they do not know the terms and conditions attached to their own products, they are unlikely to be able to help you choose the right one for you.

Asking questions
Some points to raise in your initial discussions may include:

- Are there any plans to close or expand the branch office?

- How extensive is the organisation and ATM network?

- Are there any costs involved in using other branches or another oganisation's ATM machine?

- How long does it take for a cheque to clear before I can use that money?

- What restrictions apply on withdrawing money?

- What services do you not provide?

- Are you a member of an ombudsman scheme and how does your complaints procedure work?

- What discounted or free banking services will you provide if I open an account?

Considering free gifts

A special area where caution is needed is that of 'free gifts'. Just as there are no free lunches, so it is unlikely that there are any free gifts when it comes to the provision of services by banks and building societies. Institutions offer everything from book tokens to free flights abroad to attract customers. Free gifts may be available to all new account holders, to those who fall into some special category such as students who have recently left college, or only to people who obtain associated credit cards on opening an account.

Make sure that there are no hidden charges or restrictions imposed on the accounts where such free gifts are available. It is no use obtaining a £25 book token on opening a credit card account, if the annual fee for that card is £30 and a comparable credit card account has no annual fee. The same goes for other free gifts.

ASSERTING YOUR RIGHTS

Banking code of practice

Obtaining the code
A code of practice for banks, building societies and card issuers now exists to give you guidance on the way in which these organisations should treat you. The code is drawn up by the British Bankers' Association, the Building Societies' Association and the Association for Payment Clearing Services. It is revised every few years, taking into account the comments of customers and people involved in the business. It is a voluntary code, and therefore not legally binding on banks and others, but it is accepted by them as conforming to good banking practice.

This means they would find it very difficult to justify deviating from the practices outlined in the code if their conduct became an issue in a later dispute. A copy of the code is available free from these organisations (addresses at the back of the book), or a branch of a bank or building society should be able to give you a copy or tell you where you can obtain one.

Using the code
The code is well worth reading before you begin to look for the best place to put your money. It will give you a standard against which you can judge an organisation's performance, and should assist you in any discussion with banks, building societies and other fundholders. These are just a few of the points which are useful to bear in mind and which are covered in the code:

- Banks, building societies and card issuers should be fair and reasonable and should take positive steps to help customers understand how banking services work.

- Information and advice about banking services relevant to customers should be made available upon request, at any time and in any event upon opening an account.

- Terms and conditions upon which organisations provide services should be expressed in plain language, and customers should be told how variations of those terms and conditions will be notified to them in the future.

- Summaries of the key features of common bank services should be available.

- Written summaries of charges payable in connection with services should be made available when accounts are opened and subsequently upon request.

- Details of customer complaints procedures should be available at all times.

- The customer should be given the opportunity to give instructions that they do not wish to receive marketing material at the time they open accounts.

Knowing your basic banking rights

You will acquire a variety of rights once you decide to open an account with an institution. The particular rights you acquire depend upon the detailed terms and conditions of business. These general rights will fall into a number of classes. You should be on your guard if any of these rights appear to be limited, or the subject of overly technical restrictions, when you read any material produced by banks, building societies and others.

Ensuring confidentiality
Your bank or building society must keep all information regarding any account you hold, and any other information relating to your affairs, confidential. It must not disclose any such information, except with your authority, to any third party whether that third party is a business associate, family member or investigative journalist. There is usually an implied agreement between you and

your bank that it may give credit references. If you are worried about this particular aspect of your relationship, ask for special measures to be taken.

Using reasonable care and skill

The bank is under a legal duty to use reasonable care and skill in conducting its business with you. This means it must take reasonable steps to verify facts relevant to giving you any advice. Be wary of attempts to limit legal liability in this regard. So-called 'exclusion clauses', which attempt to prevent organisations from incurring a liability to pay you damages if things go wrong, may prevent you from recovering losses incurred when a bank is at fault. If you spot such a clause, in the form of terms and conditions, do not just accept it. Ask what it means and the circumstances in which a bank or building society will seek to rely on it.

Making payments

A bank can only make payments out of your account if it receives a lawfully completed order for it to do so. Consequently, if it receives a cheque on which the signature has been forged, it cannot make that payment – even if the forgery is a good one! If it does so under the mistaken belief that it is a proper signature, you can reclaim money paid out of your account.

Additionally, if you have an account which is in credit, the bank must pay over the money to you within normal banking hours at the branch where you opened the account unless you have specifically agreed to restrictions on the circumstances of withdrawal. Be aware that a bank has a right to use a sum of money it owes to you, say the balance in your current account, to pay a debt you owe the bank such as a car loan account. Banks often refer to this as the right to 'combine' or 'set off' accounts. You may wish to keep your personal and business accounts at separate organisations. Doing so may affect your ability to obtain a loan.

Changing the contract

As time goes by, the agreement with the bank will change. For example, it may issue new terms and conditions applicable to debit or credit cards, or simply alter interest rates. It is important to check any changes, particularly changes to interest, charges and the restrictions imposed on you. The bank should publicise these prominently in circulars, and in the case of interest rates in other publicly available material such as newspaper advertisements. Such circulars affect your rights and consequently you should take careful note of them.

CASE STUDIES

Jeff wants to arrange a student loan

Jeff is 18 and about to start university. He has never had a bank account of his own before. He is arranging a student loan and intends to shop around for the best deal before opening an account. He will be on a tight budget for a few years, and is nervous about keeping control of his money as he tends to be a bit disorganised with financial matters.

Patricia flexes her financial muscle

Patricia is 24 and has just started a new job. She has a host of new plastic cards she wants to try out and a new computer to surf the Internet. She banks with Greenbank Plc who run an on-line banking service. After years of kow-towing to the bank she intends to turn the tables on her bankers now that she is earning regular money and is looking forward to calling the tune. She is currently renting accommodation and wants to buy her own place, but is worried about keeping up the mortgage payments, if she can get one. Her father is the manager of Greenbank's local branch.

John seeks new banking options

John is 40 and a director of his own furniture shop, Goodwood Limited. The company wants to increase its loan because it is expanding by opening another shop. John has been drawing heavily on his personal overdraft to finance the business, and the bank has now told him that this must stop even though he has not reached the agreed limit. He is unhappy at the way the bank has treated him and is looking around for a new bank. John is married with children and his wife works at a local school. She has just inherited a lump sum, from her recently deceased mother, which she wants to keep for the benefit of the children for whom she will open accounts. They are seeking advice on the finances of the business and the products available to invest the inheritance.

QUESTIONS AND ANSWERS

Q   *If I meet with or talk to a representative of a bank or building society, am I under any obligation to enter into any agreement with them?*

A Until you have signed a formal agreement with any organisation, you can withdraw from any discussions and you will not be liable for any costs. If any representative puts you under pressure or makes you feel uncomfortable in your discussions, you should take this as an indication that you would be better taking your custom elsewhere. It is also against the spirit of the code of good banking practice for anyone to try to pressurise you into signing any agreements. Also, if you open one account with one bank you may still obtain other services from another financial organisation if you wish.

Q *Is my money safer in a bank than in a building society or post office?*

A It is true that most high street banks are bigger than the average building society, but both types of organisation have schemes to protect investors in the event of that organisation becoming insolvent. Details of these deposit protection schemes are available from the Banking and Building Society **Ombudsmen** whose details are given at the end of the book. At the post office money invested in National Savings accounts is effectively guaranteed by the government.

Q *If I write or telephone for details of banking products to be sent to me, will I be inundated by junk mail?*

A No. Any reputable bank, building society, credit card company or other financial organisation should ask your permission first before putting you on any mailing list. If you find you are receiving junk mail, a telephone call to their head office requesting your details be removed should do the trick. If the mail continues to arrive, contact your local Trading Standards Department and they should be able to help.

DISCUSSION POINTS

1. Does the idea of planning your finances intimidate you? If so, why?

2. What points would be most important to you in deciding whether to use one bank or building society over another?

3. What questions would you most like your bank manager to answer about the way their bank works?

2
Opening an Account

CHOOSING THE RIGHT TYPE OF ACCOUNT

Once you have found a bank, building society or other organisation which you believe will provide the services you require, there are a number of other decisions which you have to make before you actually apply for an account.

Deciding whether to tie up your money

The first decision you need to make is whether you wish to put money in an account which restricts your access to it in some way. A number of accounts are available which pay a higher rate of interest, provided you give a specified number of days' written notice before making a withdrawal. The period of notice can be anything from seven days to a year. Generally, the longer the notice period the higher the rate of interest which your money will earn while it is in the account.

Checking terms for restrictions

Some of these accounts allow you to make a small number of withdrawals from the account each year at shorter notice than that specified without loss of interest. Other accounts allow you to withdraw monies from the account at short notice but penalise you by deducting interest on the amount you have withdrawn. The terms and conditions set out in full the precise restrictions imposed on withdrawing money in the account. Make sure you understand the circumstances in which you will lose interest if you have to obtain funds quickly.

If you do not want to tie up your money, consider using a current or instant access account. It may be worth having one of these accounts as well as one of the savings accounts which restrict access. Any surplus cash in the instant access or current account can be swept into the higher interest account each month just before you get paid or at some other time that suits you. These accounts are described below.

Using a current account

In the past five years current accounts have changed almost beyond recognition. They used to be available only from banks, pay no interest on money in the account (that is, credit balances) and you were charged for the privilege of keeping your money at the bank. Today current accounts are available at banks, building societies and through the financial arms of some other large retail organisations. You should be able to find a current account which offers one or more of the following features:

- no bank charges provided you keep the account in credit
- interest on credit balances although the rate is lower than savings accounts
- interest-free overdrafts at least for the first £50 borrowed on overdraft
- telephone banking
- on-line or computerised banking
- cash cards.

You will be able to obtain higher rates of interest on some of the accounts described later in this section. A current account is, for example, a useful place to have your salary paid into at first. You can pay bills from it then transfer any sums you do not need straightaway into one of the other accounts which pays a better rate of interest.

Finding a higher rate of interest

Using a deposit account
A **deposit account** is an account which offers a higher rate of interest on credit balances but which does not usually offer a cheque book or services such as money transfer (see page 72). Some deposit accounts come with a cash card so that you can withdraw monies through an ATM. There are a number of different types of deposit account such as fixed term deposits (which may require you to lock up your money for up to five years) and the various fixed and variable interest rate accounts. The conditions which may apply to these accounts vary widely. The main points you should check are set out below.

Giving notice
Find out how much notice you need to give before you can withdraw any money in the account without losing any interest.

Maintaining a minimum balance
Some higher interest accounts require you to maintain a minimum balance in order to earn interest at the higher rate. Others have sliding scales where interest increases in small increments depending on how much money you have in the account at any time.

Fixing the rate of interest
If you believe that interest rates will fall in the future you can consider placing your savings in an account which guarantees a fixed rate of return regardless of what happens to interest rates generally. These accounts are attractive if you want to be sure of a stable income from a capital sum. A lot of fixed interest accounts also require you to leave your money on deposit for a relatively long period, normally between one and five years. There are some deposit accounts available which try to give you the best of both worlds. These will offer a minimum rate of return but will give you the benefit of any increase in the level of interest rates generally by varying the rate upwards to follow economic trends. In every case it is for you to decide whether or not you are prepared to take the risk of fixing the rate of interest you earn on your savings.

Receiving interest periodically
The way in which interest is paid to you can be important, as well as the rate. The best way to illustrate the point is by way of a simple example. Assume you invest £10,000 in an account which pays interest at 5 per cent. Compare the amount you have at the end of a year where the interest is paid to you monthly, half-yearly and annually (ignoring tax which we will assume is neutral across the three choices):

Amount invested	Total interest paid	Balance at year end
£10,000 (interest annual)	£500.00	£10,500.00
£10,000 (interest quarterly)	£509.45	£10,509.45
£10,000 (interest monthly)	£511.62	£10,511.62

The frequency with which interest is credited to your account throughout the year does have a small effect on the amount you earn.

Paying tax
Unless you invest in an account which is specially exempted from the income tax regime you will pay tax on any interest you earn.

Banks and building societies will normally deduct tax from the interest they pay you at the basic rate. This is what is meant when they advertise interest paid **net of tax**. If you are a higher rate tax payer, you will have to pay the balance of tax due on the amount you have received. Similarly, if you receive interest **gross of tax**, you will be liable to meet any tax at basic and higher rates which may be payable on it. If you do not pay tax you can obtain a form from your bank or building society which when completed allows them to pay interest to you without deducting basic rate tax.

The following types of account are normally exempt from taxation of interest and so are correctly described as paying tax free interest:

- Tax Exempt Special Savings Accounts or TESSAs
- National Savings accounts
- offshore savings accounts of banks and building societies

COMPLETING OPENING FORMALITIES

Taking identification
Whenever an account is opened the organisation with whom the account will be held will require you to produce evidence proving your:

- name
- address
- occupation.

Apart from the obvious desire to know who it is dealing with, the bank or building society has to go through these formalities in order to obtain certain technical protections under banking legislation. For people who are investing large sums of money more stringent identification procedures now have to be followed by financial services organisations, in order to comply with the legislation designed to prevent money laundering.

The type of identification documents which will be required are one or more of the following:

- passport
- driving licence
- identification cards with signatures
- for business: partnership agreements
- for companies: certificates of incorporation.

Providing references

Some organisations will want you to give them the names of two referees who will vouch for your good reputation. Again, part of the reason for taking up references is that it affords the organisation certain technical protections under banking laws. Details of your employer will normally suffice, along with one other independent person who knows you well.

Signing a mandate form

In order to open an account you will need to sign a **mandate** or authority form. This gives the bank specimens of your signature and authorises them to make debits and credits to your account against documents (cheques, paying-in slips, letters) carrying that signature. It also allows the bank to operate the account in accordance with its standard terms and conditions as amended from time to time.

Operating joint accounts

There is a common misconception that only those whose name appears on the account can make withdrawals from it. In fact anyone who has signed a mandate form in relation to that account can do so. For example, someone who is elderly and not as mobile as they used to be may wish to nominate a son or daughter as an authorised signatory on their account in order to transact business on their behalf. Only people who you wish to authorise to make withdrawals should sign the mandate form for your account. You can also specify that for amounts above a certain limit more than one authorised signatory must sign any instruction to the bank.

Making your first withdrawals

There is normally a delay between opening an account and being able to write cheques on it or make cash withdrawals from it. The bank will want to clear any cheque you have paid in to open the account and complete the process of taking up references. It will also have to arrange for cheque guarantee, ATM/cash cards and cheque books to be printed with your details on them. The extent of the delay varies, but you should expect it to take about ten days and make special arrangements if you need to call upon the money in the account earlier.

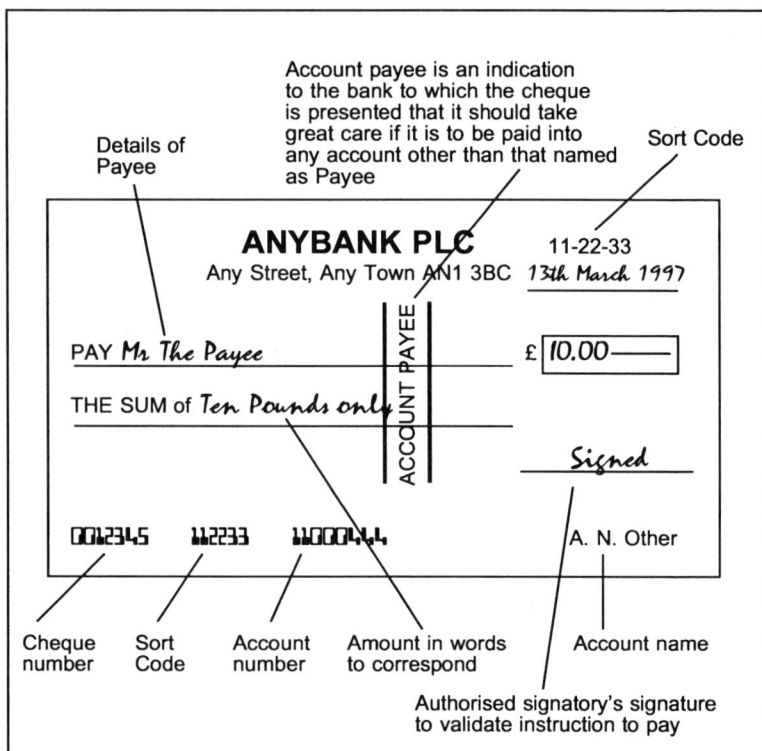

Fig. 2. Details on a cheque are an instruction to your bank.

USING A CHEQUE BOOK

Writing a cheque

A cheque is just an instruction to your bank to make payment of a sum of money to the person named on the cheque from your account. The following is an explanation of some of the jargon you may come across, and some tips on security when issuing cheques in payment for goods and services.

The drawer

The person on whose account the cheque is written is called the **drawer** of the cheque. The people who are authorised to sign cheques on the drawer's account are known as authorised signatories to that account.

The payee
The **payee** is the person to whom the cheque is made out.

The date
A cheque should be dated on the day it is written. Sometimes a cheque is said to be post-dated. This means that it cannot be paid in by the payee before that date. A bank or other organisation need not honour a post-dated cheque even if there were funds in the account at the time it was written.

Signing
It is important to ensure that you make your signature distinctive so that it is not easily forged. Having said that, you must use your normal signature. If you have handwriting which is easily copied, think about including a middle name or initial in your signature when signing the bank mandate form. This will make it more difficult for someone to take your signature (which excludes this detail on an ordinary letter) and forge it on cheques.

Amount in figures and words
The cheque requires the amount to be stated in figures and words. If the two do not correspond the cheque will be sent back to you for correction and representation by the payee. Make sure that the box containing the figures is full, no matter how small an amount the cheque is for, as the commonest cheque fraud is to add noughts on the end or move the decimal point! *Never* sign a cheque and leave the amount to be filled in later by the payee. You will have no claim against the bank on which the cheque is drawn when it honours such a cheque.

Obtaining money from other banks
You can withdraw funds from your own branch at any time without providing additional identification. In order to obtain funds from a different branch of your bank, or from a different bank, you will need to write a cheque and present a **cheque guarantee card**. This states that the bank where you hold the account guarantees that it will meet a cheque in an amount equal to, or smaller than, the amount stated on the card (usually £50 or £100) whether or not there are actually funds in that account. This gives the third party bank the security it needs to give you cash. The same applies when you use a cheque to pay for goods in a shop.

Note that cheque guarantee cards limit the bank's obligation to meet a cheque to £50 or £100 per transaction. You should not write two cheques for £50 to pay for one item of goods worth £100 using a cheque guarantee card. If the bank spots that there was only one transaction but two cheques, it need not honour them if there are no funds in the account.

MAKING REGULAR PAYMENTS FROM YOUR ACCOUNT

Using standing orders
A **standing order** is an instruction to your bank or building society to make a payment of a certain amount on a specified day each month (or week, or year) to a third party.

A standing order is essentially no different from any other instruction you may give your bank to pay funds out of your account.

If the date on which you wish the payment to be made or the amount of the payment alters you should give your bank at least three working days' notice to enable them to make the necessary amendments. Most banks and building societies have special forms which they use to set up standing orders and these should be used whenever possible. However, if you need to cancel a standing order you can do this by simply telephoning the bank and confirming the cancellation by letter at a later date.

Authorising direct debits
A **direct debit** is completely different from a standing order. With a standing order *you* tell the bank how much to pay and when. With a direct debit you authorise a *third party* to tell your bank how much to pay to them and when. The company to which the payment is to be made will ask you to complete a direct debit form which you return to it. The form will contain details of the account from which the payment is to be made and the period during which the payments may be made. The form contains an instruction by you to your bank or building society to make payments as from time to time required by the third party.

Direct debits are used where the amount of the regular payments may vary from time to time.

For example, you would use direct debit where you are repaying a loan and the interest rate on it varies from month to month. Only certain approved organisations may use direct debits and they have to undertake to:

• inform their customer of any change in the amount taken from the account

• notify you if the date on which the payment is taken changes

• indemnify you and the bank or building society against loss occasioned by making incorrect payments under the system.

Direct debits do cause concern from time to time. However, the number of complaints in relation to the number of transactions effected by direct debits is very small. The vast majority of direct debit users are satisfied. Most complaints involve people who, having signed direct debit forms, change their minds about using this method of payment and then find that one or more payments have been mistakenly taken from their accounts. Clerical error, rather than actual dishonesty, seems to be the cause of most complaints and the indemnities described above compensate people in most cases. Do not be afraid to use direct debits.

Cancelling a direct debit instruction
You can cancel a direct debit over the telephone by instructing your bank not to make any further payments to the organisation in whose favour you signed a direct debit authority. You should write to both the party who holds the direct debit form from you and your bank to ensure that both parties are aware of your wish to stop the payments.

Paying by credit transfer
Payments can be made from your account by **credit transfer**, also known as **bank giro credit**. You have probably seen the forms used for this type of transfer as most telephone, gas and electricity companies attach such forms to their bills. By completing the relevant account details and taking it along to your branch you can send money to pay the bill without having to write a cheque. Of course, in the case of domestic bills you can also use such forms to accompany your cheque in payment of the bill and as a form of remittance advice.

MAINTAINING YOUR ACCOUNT

Knowing the difference between credit and debit

Bankers talk about accounts being credited or debited with sums or having credit or debit balances. If you are to maintain your account you need to know what these terms mean.

Crediting an account

This means entering a payment into an account. When you pay a cheque into your account the amount of the cheque is credited to your account.

Credit balance

An account has a credit balance when there are funds in the account. If you are not overdrawn on your account the account has a credit balance.

Debiting an account

An account is debited every time a sum is paid out of the account. Each time you write a cheque to pay for something and that cheque is presented for payment by the shop your account is debited with the amount of the cheque. Bank charges and interest payable by you to the bank will be debited to or paid from your account.

Debit balance

A debit balance means you are overdrawn. You owe the bank the amount of the debit balance on your account.

Checking statements

It is vitally important that once you receive a statement showing transactions on your account you check it against your own records to ensure it is correct. The statement is taken as good but not conclusive evidence of the state of your account in any dispute. If you have not checked it and notified a representative of the organisation of any discrepancy, you may later have difficulty establishing that the bank made an error. There is no case law which states that you are prevented from arguing over a mistake at a later date, but it will be difficult to prove you have not been at fault in not checking your statement. The sooner you notify someone of an error the stronger your position will be in any dispute.

Keeping records

You will only be able to keep track of your account if you maintain an independent record of payments made into and out of your account. Both cheque books and paying-in books have stubs which you can complete to ensure you have a record of transactions on the account. Get into the habit of completing these stubs, as banks and building societies do make mistakes.

Keeping records on computer

There are a number of computer programs available to help you keep track of your finances. Microsoft Money and Quicken are two of the most popular ones. These programs, or any spreadsheet program, will take the pain out of the maths of keeping track of your bank balance, at least for the computer literate.

The advantage of these programs is that they avoid the need for you to recalculate manually the balance on your account every time you have a sum credited or debited to your account. Provided each sum you pay into and out of your account is keyed into the program (along with whatever other details you want to keep) the program ensures you can view an up-to-date statement of your account at any time. Once periodic payments into and out of the account are keyed in, the programs will add or subtract the relevant amounts automatically. Some of these programs allow you to link to the bank itself to download information. More is said about this type of service in Chapter 5.

Clearing payments

One of the commonest causes of complaint between customers and their banks is the charges levied by banks for unauthorised overdrafts. There is more on this subject in the next chapter. Remember that the time it takes to clear a payment into your account is longer than the time it takes for the bank to debit your account with a withdrawal. A cheque paid into your account can take from one to nine days to clear, that is to be credited to your account. A payment out of your account by ATM, or by debit card payments such as Switch or Delta, will usually take no longer than three days to show up on your account and may show immediately.

Unless your bank or building society gives you a free overdraft, or you have arranged an overdraft to cover these timing differences, you could find yourself out of pocket. Even if you do not think you need an overdraft it is worth organising some limited facility to cover this.

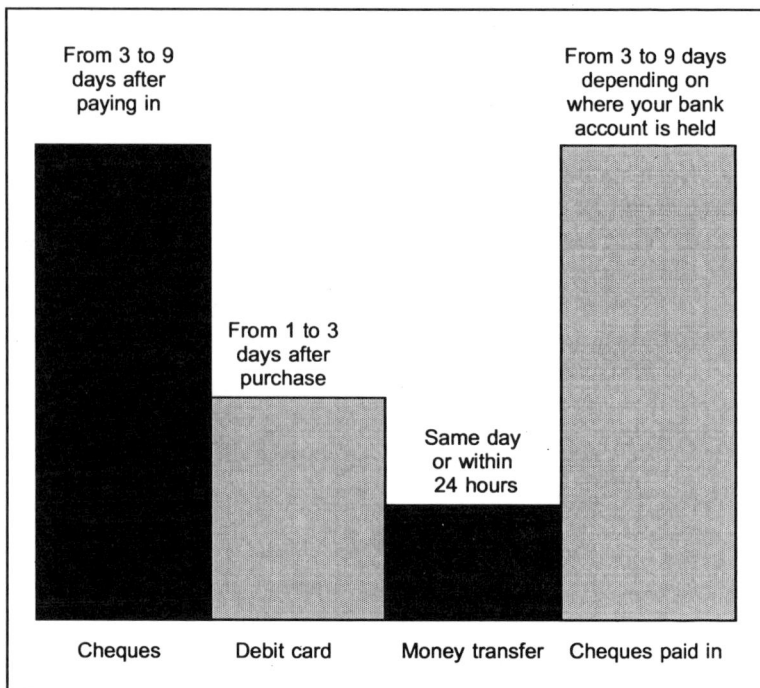

Fig. 3. How cheques, debit cards and money transfers
are processed.

OPENING AN ACCOUNT FOR CHILDREN

Teaching children about money

One of the best ways to educate children early on about money is to let them have their own account to manage. Depending on the age of the child, he or she will be able to run the account with a fair degree of independence. The following section details the position adopted by banks and building societies when opening accounts for children in different age groups. Before you arrange for the account to be opened think about what you would like your child to learn from the experience:

• budgeting
• saving
• dealing with other people
• how to look for the best deal for your money.

Most organisations try to attract young customers with free gifts.

There may be an opportunity to teach the account holder that 'free' gifts may sometimes come at a price ... such as a lower interest rate!

Contracting as a minor
Until a person reaches the age of 18 he or she is classified as a minor. Minors are unable to enter into legally binding agreements, and consequently banks and building societies take particular care when dealing with children. For children under the age of 7 it is usual for the account to be opened in the name of the parent or guardian with a note that the account is 're a child'. For older children the account can be in their own name but some organisations will insist on operating the account in credit. That is, they will not allow a minor to become overdrawn unless:

• a parent or someone else guarantees the account

• they obtain confirmation of an employer's payment of wages into the account on a regular basis.

Working out the tax position
By and large children are treated as separately taxable people with their own personal allowances. However, in some cases the Inland Revenue is able to treat the income earned on money invested for children by parents as income of the parent for tax purposes. If money invested by a parent for a child earns more than £100 in any year the excess over that sum is treated as being income of the parent for the purposes of paying tax. In the case of children who have no other taxable income it is well worth considering those accounts which pay interest gross or free of tax so that it does not get automatically deducted and have to be claimed back later. National Savings accounts fall into the latter category and are very popular as children's accounts.

Considering free gifts
As seen in the last chapter, the brightly coloured pass books and free toys often go hand-in-hand with lower rates of return on money invested.

CASE STUDIES

Jeff decides to become organised
Jeff knows that his income for the next few years will consist of lump

sums contributed by his parents and through the student loan scheme. He decides that he will put the bulk of the money in a building society high interest account where he must give thirty days' notice of withdrawal. He will put a smaller sum in an instant access account which pays a lower rate of interest. He realises that he will have to be more orderly in calling for withdrawals of lump sums from the high interest account. He knows though, that even if he gives notice late interest will still be credited at the lower instant access rate. Jeff had checked the terms and conditions to ensure he would not forgo all interest in such circumstances.

Patricia saves for a deposit

Patricia has her wages paid into her current account with Greenbank Plc. The current account pays only a small rate of interest on credit balances. Patricia decides to use the on-line banking facility to instruct her bank to move any credit balance in her account to a fixed interest deposit account on the last day of each month. Because she was an existing customer who had previously shown Greenbank her passport as identification, she was able to open this account with them on-line for that purpose. Although the deposit account does not have a cheque book, she is happy to continue paying bills via the computer service or writing what few cheques she needs on her current account.

John is turned away

John is unhappy with his existing bank and the service it has provided. He meets with the manager of a small building society who has just set up a branch in his town. John wants to move his personal and business loans to the building society. The manager tells him they do not make loans to businesses, although they would be happy to open a personal account for him. John believes that if he moves his personal account the bank may be less willing to make further business loans to him and so, for the moment, is forced to stay where he is.

John's wife decides to open children's accounts with the building society. Adam, her youngest son is 7 so she opens an account in her name but it is designated 're Adam R...'. Her elder son is 14 and, although a minor, the building society allows him to open an account in his own name provided he agrees to keep it in credit.

QUESTIONS AND ANSWERS

Q   *If I need to obtain money from an account which has a thirty-day* *or longer notice period, can I do so?*

A   Yes. However, you will lose some or all of the interest which
     has been earned on the amount you wish to withdraw over the
     prior thirty-day (or longer) period. Some organisations will
     give you interest for that period but at lower instant access or
     current account rates. It is important to check the exact terms
     and conditions governing early withdrawals.

Q   *What should I do if I spot an error on my statement?*

A   First telephone your bank, building society or financial
     organisation and tell them about the error. Follow their
     advice on how you should deal with the matter. However,
     always make a note of your telephone call and follow it up with
     a letter to the relevant branch official or the manager. Never sit
     on a mistake believing the bank will put it right next time – it
     may not. The sooner you alert the branch to their mistake, and
     the better your written records of the action you took, the
     stronger your position will be in any later dispute.

Q   *How do I stop a cheque I have written from being paid?*

A   To stop a cheque you must inform your bank before it has been
     presented for payment, ie, before the payee has paid it into their
     account. After presentation a bank only has one day in which it
     may stop the transfer of funds to the payee. You should
     telephone your bank to instruct them to stop payment and
     follow this up with a written instruction by post or fax.

DISCUSSION POINTS

1.   Is a high interest savings account the only form of saving
     investment you will consider, or is with-profits insurance, unit
     trusts or some other investment going to serve you better?

2.   How will you monitor your finances?

3.   What are the lessons you would like your children to learn from
     any account you open for them?

3
Borrowing Money

CALCULATING THE COST OF BORROWING

Costing your loan

For some people the cost of a loan means the amount of interest payable to the lender, in return for the use of the money borrowed over the lifetime of the loan. However, it is wise to investigate matters a little more closely before agreeing to borrow money.

This section looks at some of the factors you should take into account in deciding which lender is offering the best deal. Lenders are obliged by the **Consumer Credit Act** to make clear exactly what the cost of borrowing will be to their customers. More is said in the next chapter about the valuable rights conferred by the Act on borrowers, people buying on hire purchase terms or entering into other credit agreements. Similar provisions apply to personal loans.

Paying interest

Opting for fixed or variable rate
Most loans have a variable rate of interest which is tied to the level of interest rates generally set by the Bank of England. This rate is referred to as bank **base rate** (it used to be called minimum lending rate). Base rates may move up or down over the lifetime of a loan, increasing or reducing the amount you have to pay in interest. Your lender's agreement must specify that it can vary the rate and it must notify you of any changes. This is usually done by advertising the change in newspapers and sending customers a formal notice of change in the interest rate.

Some lenders offer to lend money at fixed rates of interest, so that you can assess at the outset what the entire cost in interest payments will be. People find this attractive as it enables them to budget for the loan repayments very accurately. If you wish to borrow you need to assess how you believe interest rates will move over the expected life of the loan. If you expect them to move higher than the fixed rate being offered the decision is easy: fix the rate.

Capitalising interest
One of the points which is often overlooked by potential borrowers is the time at which the lender adds interest to the amount of the loan. If interest from month one is added to the amount of the loan, and interest charged in month two on the new outstanding amount (capital plus interest from month one), the level of effective interest payable has moved up. An example may help:

> Loan: £10,000 at an interest rate of 12 per cent.
> Month 1: interest is equal to £100. The calculation is made as follows: £10,000 is divided by 100 to give 1 per cent. The figure is multiplied by the rate of interest, which happens to be 12, and then divided by 12 to give the amount due for one month.
> The lender adds the interest to the capital and calculates the interest for month 2 on £10,100.
> [Month 2: Interest is equal to £101.]
> Most lenders will go through this process quarterly rather than monthly.

The lender is obliged to show what is known as the **Annual Percentage Rate** (abbreviated to **APR**) for loans. This gives you the effective rate of interest over one year taking account, amongst other things, of the type of timing differences described here. Details of all the charges being made should be clearly shown in the documents given to you.

Default interest
If you are late in making a payment to your lender the agreement may allow the lender to charge a higher rate of interest on the amount due but unpaid. With some lenders if you are even a day late this higher rate default interest may be charged for a whole month, or possibly longer depending on the terms of the agreement. If you know that there may be occasion when you are going to be slightly late with repayments, and you still believe that you can otherwise afford to borrow money, you will need to budget for these costs.

Paying fees when borrowing
The charges levied by lenders for setting up an overdraft or personal loan should be included in your calculation of the cost to you of borrowing the money.

Paying an initial fee

Lenders commonly charge an initial fee for making a loan or overdraft facility. This charge is sometimes called an arrangement fee. It really makes no difference to you what it is called because it is a sum you have to pay in order to obtain the loan. Let's return to the example of borrowing £10,000 over one year. If bank A offers the loan at 12 per cent with no fee, is it better to go to building society B where you can get the loan at 10 per cent but have to pay an arrangement fee of 3 per cent of the amount of the loan? Assuming both organisations capitalise interest at the same time, to make things easier, the amounts payable are as follows:

Amount	Bank A	Building society B
Capital	£10,000	£10,000
Interest	£1,200	£1,000
Fee	nil	£500
Total	**£11,200**	**£11,500**

If the loan was taken over a period of more than a year, the difference in the cost between a loan at a lower rate of interest, but with an initial fee, and a loan at a higher rate, reduces. Eventually the lower rate loan becomes the cheaper option. In the example this would be the case if the loan was taken over a three-year period.

Paying an annual fee

The same principle applies to annual or even monthly fees which may be payable to a lender. You need to weigh up whether the lower rate of interest plus the fee costs more than simply paying the higher rate of interest. One sector in which fees can be important in determining the cost of borrowing is with credit and charge cards.

Paying for insurance

A lot of lenders now sell credit insurance to their borrowers. This is where you pay a small premium, usually monthly, which insures you against becoming unable to repay the debt through some unforeseen circumstance such as illness or losing your job. The premium is usually calculated as a small percentage of the amount outstanding to the lender, though other bases of calculating the premium do exist. Some lenders make such insurance a mandatory requirement for loans over a certain size.

You may be grateful for the peace of mind such insurance brings you in which case, provided you do not already carry that type of insurance (do you already have critical illness cover, for example) or could not get it cheaper elsewhere, you can write the cost off as money well spent. If, however, you are forced into buying such insurance because it is a condition of the lender making the money available and you do not really need it, the cost of the premiums is simply another cost to you of buying the use of the lender's money.

Who benefits from the insurance?
It is worth spending some time checking who ultimately benefits from this type of insurance. If you are unfortunate enough to find yourself in a position to default on a loan and the insurers pay out, the money will be paid to the lender. That much is fine. However, always check whether in those circumstances the insurer may reclaim any monies it has paid under the policy to the lender from you. If once the insurance company has paid your lender, it has a claim for a similar amount against you, all you have done by taking out the insurance and paying the premiums is to swap the identity of your lender! Is that a privilege you want to pay for or something you would rather do without?

What is covered?
Additionally, the exact benefits paid should be investigated. For example some insurance will pay the loan instalments for the first six months of any period of illness or unemployment, but will not cover any further periods. As with any matter concerning insurance, if you are told something about the extent of the cover provided, make a note and try to get confirmation in writing. It may help in any argument later.

Repaying a loan early
When borrowing money it is wise to check what the position is if you repay the loan earlier than the agreed final repayment date. Sometimes loan agreements allow lenders to charge an early repayment premium in the form of a one-off lump sum payment if the borrower wishes to repay the loan early. This type of clause is particularly common in home loans. The justification for such early repayment premiums is said to be the initial costs incurred by the lender in allocating the funds for the loan, and the fact that the level of interest rate was set upon the loan being repaid over a longer period.

Moneylenders
Banks and building societies are not the only organisations which

lend money. In the UK there is a thriving moneylender trade carried on by registered moneylenders who even have their own trade association. The terms on which these moneylenders carry out business differ in important respects from those of banks and building societies. The main differences are:

- Interest rates are usually much higher and can reach astronomical levels as rates of 150 per cent or more are common.

- The lender may call to receive weekly or monthly repayments.

- The sums borrowed may be smaller than any bank or other mainstream lender would consider.

- There may be additional costs over and above the interest rate charged on the loan.

Whilst some such companies are very large, well managed and respected, it pays to be particularly vigilant when dealing with such moneylenders. Check their agreements and get written confirmation of the arrangements you are entering into, including the penalties payable should you default on repayments.

There are also companies and individuals who set themselves up as, effectively, lenders of the last resort. They tend to be the lenders who people turn to when no other source of funding is available. In popular terms they are loan sharks, and the name says it all. They are to be avoided.

ARRANGING AN OVERDRAFT

Understanding overdrafts

An overdraft is a loan facility which is designed to meet temporary shortfalls in the cash you would otherwise have available. It is important to understand that, unless a lender has specifically agreed otherwise, an overdraft is repayable immediately upon demand being made by the lender. In this context 'immediately' means allowing only time for you to effect the mechanics of payment (eg, go to the bank to pay money in), not some 'reasonable' period of days. Most lenders who provide overdrafts operate them on the basis that they renew them each year unless the account has been maintained improperly and that a day or two is given for repaying them.

Paying for an overdraft

The lender will from time to time charge interest on the amount outstanding on the overdraft. Usually the interest accrues on a daily basis so you are only paying interest for the days you are actually overdrawn. (You need to check that interest is not charged for any longer period.) However, there will be some other costs involved.

Arrangement fee

This is the initial charge for setting up the overdraft and may be made each time the overdraft facility is renewed. We have already seen that such fees can make a great difference to the cost of borrowing.

Monthly fees

Some lenders charge additional fees which may be levied monthly or over some longer period if you actually use the overdraft facility. So even if you are overdrawn for just one day this fee may become payable. Some lenders off a 'free' overdraft facility provided that you are overdrawn for less than a certain number of days in the month. By this they usually mean that no additional fee will be payable. For people who are only usually overdrawn for a few days each month this type of free overdraft can save quite a bit of money over a year.

Daily fees

A few years ago most of the larger high street lenders took steps to discourage what was then a relatively common practice of going overdrawn when you had not arranged a formal overdraft limit, or exceeding the limit of an agreed overdraft. They had always charged a higher rate of interest on such accounts to customers and some lenders levied a flat rate fee. Now it is likely that you will incur higher interest costs, plus a daily fee which can be as much as £3 to £9 per day, if you run up an unauthorised overdraft or go over your overdraft limit. Unauthorised overdrafts are not the most cost effective way of borrowing money and should be avoided altogether.

Agreeing an overdraft limit

Even if you do not expect to have to borrow money, it is worth setting up a small overdraft facility to ensure that you do not end up paying the fees for unauthorised overdrafts. Most banks and building societies offer new customers some sort of an overdraft facility if they are asked when the account is opened. If the organisation you bank with has a telephone banking service, you can generally obtain small overdrafts or small increases in your overdraft limit over the telephone quite quickly. For larger overdrafts the procedure you have to follow is like that when you are applying for a personal loan.

APPLYING FOR A PERSONAL LOAN

Understanding how lenders look at loan applications

What criteria do lenders apply when they are considering a request for a loan? As a preliminary point, most banks and building societies will only consider certain personal loans if you already have an account with them or are prepared to move your existing accounts to them.

Credit scoring

Most lenders operate a system of credit scoring. Each customer is assessed in relation to a number of factors such as:

- Is the home owned rather than rented?
- How long has the applicant been resident at the present address?
- How long has the applicant been with the current employer?
- What is the applicant's income?
- What are the applicant's outgoings?
- What is the applicant's payment record in relation to other loans?

A score is attributed to each of these factors, based on a time-tested formula about which there is much secrecy in the banking industry. The lender will be looking for factors which show stability in the applicant, such as a long record with the current employer or a long time at the current address. If you have just changed job or address, it is essential you tell the lender the reasons so that he gets the right impression of you. A good payment record on any borrowings you have had in the past is one of the most important indicators for a prospective lender.

Knowing about credit reference agencies

Lenders often take out credit references from specialist credit reference agencies before they make a loan. If you believe that there has been some problem over your credit reference, you can apply under the Data Protection Act to obtain details of any records about you which are kept in computerised form. You will have to pay a small fee to obtain copies of any entries but you will be entitled to have any misleading or inaccurate data corrected. In certain circumstances you can also obtain compensation for damage suffered as a result of an error in your records.

One word of caution. The ability to obtain compensation does not entitle you to sue a credit reference agency or a lender for the amount of the loan which you might have obtained had the reference not been in error. At best you would probably only be entitled to wasted costs involved in applying for the loan.

Trusting the customer
One of the fundamental principles which a lender applies to any application is to refuse to lend if there is any doubt at all over the integrity of the applicant for a loan. It is crucial that you make full and frank disclosure to your prospective lender of all the information which it requests during the application procedure. You can be sure that if the lender finds that the facts on the application form do not tell the whole story, it will not make the loan. If it has made the loan based on an incomplete or inaccurate application, it may be entitled to recover the loan early.

Lending for a purpose
The lender will normally want to know what the money will be used for. You can obtain loans without specifying a purpose, but these will be harder to come by if the amount requested is significant when compared to the credit balances on your account with the lender. A lender is going to be much more relaxed about making a home improvement loan which will increase the value of the property over which it has already taken a mortgage, than a loan to top up your holiday fund.

Assessing your cashflow
The lender will want to make sure that you are able to meet the loan repayments in a timely manner. Consequently they may be concerned if your income fluctuates over the year, for example if you are self-employed and income is seasonal. The amount of your disposable income must be sufficient each month (or quarter) to allow the loan to be repaid on time.

Giving security
For some loans lenders will insist on having some form of **security**, or a **guarantee** from a third party. This gives them additional comfort that if you default they have recourse either to some asset,

in the case of security, or some other person in the case of a guarantee. Generally, secured loans should be cheaper in terms of the interest rate than unsecured loans, to reflect the lesser risk taken by the lender.

UNDERSTANDING MORTGAGES

Borrowing on security of a mortgage

For larger loans, particularly but not exclusively those to purchase a house or flat, the lender will require that the property owned or to be bought by the borrower be **charged** or **mortgaged** to it as security. (There is a technical legal difference between charge and mortgage, the details of which need not trouble you.) This means that if the loan is not repaid on time the lender can enforce the mortgage or charge, usually but not exclusively by way of a sale, to repay the loan.

Enforcing a mortgage
A lender whose borrower defaults on such a loan can:

- Sell the property to produce a sum to repay the loan either in whole or in part. If the sale proceeds, after the costs of the lender in organising the sale have been paid, are insufficient to repay the loan, he may sue the borrower for the unpaid portion. If the net sale proceeds are more than enough to repay the loan, the balance is paid to the borrower (if there is more than one mortgagee, the second in line gets the balance to apply against its loan).

- Take possession of the property, either to sell or possibly rent it out to produce an income stream from which the loan will be repaid.

- Foreclose on the property, in which case the mortgagor's interest in the property ceases to exist (irrespective of the property's value) and the mortgagee becomes the full legal owner. This remedy is used very infrequently by lender mortgagees nowadays because it can cause injustice to borrowers and consequently requires a special court order.

A mortgagee owes a duty to its borrower upon enforcement to take reasonable care to produce the best returns from the property which is the subject of the mortgage.

Chapter 9 contains some guidance on what to do if you find that you are having difficulty in repaying a loan and fear that your mortgagee may seek to enforce its security.

Choosing the right type of mortgage

There are many different types of mortgage available. The following section describes briefly the basic features of the more common mortgages. The remedies available to the lender mortgagee described above apply to all of these types of mortgages.

Ordinary repayment mortgages
This type of mortgage obliges the borrower to repay a monthly instalment which comprises partly interest and partly capital, throughout the lifetime of the loan. At the outset the major part of each monthly payment consists of interest and a small amount of capital. Gradually, as more capital is repaid, the proportion of interest in each monthly payment becomes smaller and the element of capital repaid correspondingly bigger.

Mortgages and endowment insurance policies
In this case the borrower takes out an **endowment insurance** policy which has a maturity date the same as the repayment date for the mortgage loan. The sum payable by the insurance company upon maturity of the policy is used to pay the capital sum due to the lender. The borrower pays an instalment comprising only interest each month to the lender, and a monthly or annual insurance premium to the provider of the insurance policy.

In recent years there has been considerable concern that endowment policies used in these circumstances may not generate sufficient returns to pay off the full amount of the capital sum due to the lender. Like any other investment these returns depend on the state of the economy generally. It remains to be seen whether this will cause real hardship in a large number of cases.

Pension-linked mortgages
This type of mortgage is very similar to the endowment mortgage. The borrower pays interest throughout the lifetime of the loan in the same way. The borrower also makes payments into a pension plan which will provide a lump sum to pay off the capital amount due to the lender. In addition the pension plan will produce a tax-free lump sum to provide for the borrower upon retirement. More is said about pensions in Chapter 6.

Unit trust-linked mortgages
These are the same as endowment-linked mortgages, except that the borrower pays sums into a unit trust scheme which it is hoped will

produce a capital sum sufficient to pay off the loan upon maturity. Again monthly instalments are paid to the lender, comprising interest only.

Completing mortgage formalities

Once a mortgage has been signed, it has to be registered at H M Land Registry. This can take up to a couple of months to complete, although usually the process takes place after you have moved into the property. A fee will be payable for registering the mortgage, dependent upon the amount borrowed. For people who are taking out a loan to buy a property, only one fee based on the purchase price of the property is payable. The fees are changed regularly, but details of the currently applicable fees are available from your solicitor or from the Land Registry (see Useful Addresses).

Obtaining tax relief

Basic rate tax relief is currently available on the interest paid on the first £30,000 of any mortgage. The relief is only available on the main home, not for example on loans for properties to use as holiday homes. Higher rate tax payers cannot claim any further relief.

OBTAINING A STUDENT LOAN

Deciding whether you are eligible for a loan

Student loans were introduced seven years ago. In order to be eligible for a loan you need to be both of the following.

- A home student. That is, a student who would be entitled to a mandatory education grant award from the relevant local education authority.

- Taking up a place on an eligible course. These are higher education courses, below the level of postgraduate studies, run by a publicly funded higher education establishment such as a university or college. Certain NHS courses are certified as being eligible courses by the Department of Education.

Provided you are a home student and you will be on an eligible course, you can apply for a student loan. In assessing whether to make the loan, the income you have from your parents, any grant and other sources will generally be ignored. Any earlier loans under the scheme will not be taken into account unless you still owe money or are otherwise in breach of the terms of those earlier loans.

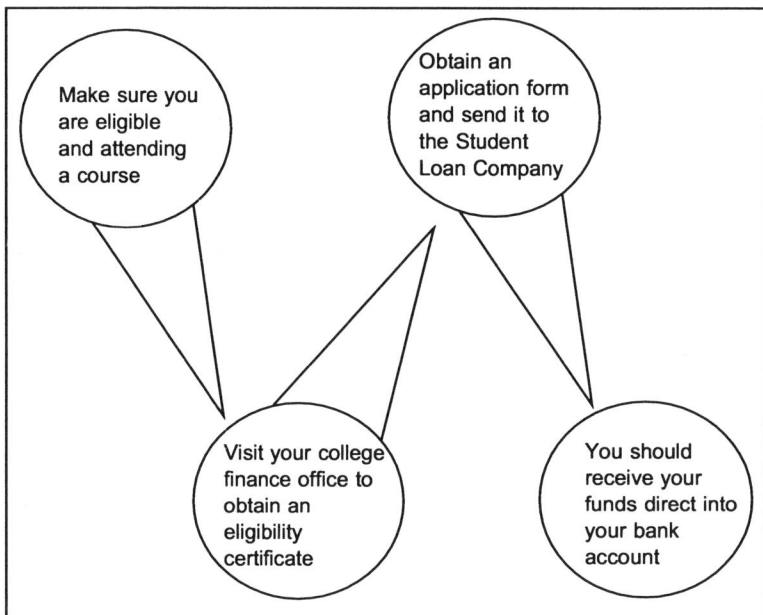

Fig. 4. Four steps to obtaining student loans.

Making an application

You can make an application for a student loan at any time during the academic year but you must actually be attending a course. Only one application can be made each academic year.

Applications are made through the college or university you are attending. They will help you fill in an application form and send it off to the Student Loan Company Limited. Details of the company appear in Useful Addresses.

Attending at the college office

You will need to take the following documents with you when you go to the relevant office at the college or university you are attending:

• your birth certificate

• proof of your bank or building society account number and sort code

- any letter from your award-making body that says you are to get an LEA mandatory award, a student's allowance from the Student Awards Agency for Scotland (SAAS), a Northern Ireland mandatory award or an NHS or DH bursary. You are also eligible if you get a DHSS bursary in Northern Ireland.

If you are eligible, your college will ask you to fill in an eligibility certificate. Your college will then authorise the certificate and send it to the Student Loan Company. Your college will give you an application form for a loan which you have to complete and send to the Student Loan Company. They will match your application with the eligibility certificate and send you a loan agreement.

The terms of the loan
The loans are index-linked to take account of inflation. Your loan will be subject to an interest charge. The rate of interest is variable and is linked to the increase in the cost of living (as shown in the Retail Price Index). The main terms are as follows:

- At present, most borrowers pay back their loan over five to seven years.

- You can pay back your loan early if you want without any additional payment.

- Once they start, repayments are made monthly. The amounts of the repayments increase each year to take account of inflation as described above.

- Repayments usually start in the April after your course finishes or you stop attending it. If you withdraw from a course but immediately start another eligible course at the same college, repayments will not start until the April after you finish (or stop attending) the latter course.

- As long as you are not behind with your loan repayments, any amount remaining due under your credit agreement will be cancelled after twenty-five years or when you reach the age of 50, whichever is earlier.

- If you die, any amount remaining due under your credit agreement is cancelled.

- The APR is 3.5 per cent.

- Once our loan is due to be repaid, you can ask to delay repaying your loan for twelve months.

CASE STUDIES

Jeff applies for a student loan

On his first day at university Jeff goes to the Student Finance Department office to obtain an eligibility certificate. He takes with him details of his instant access account including the account number, sort code and branch address. He also takes along his passport and enrolment documents as additional identification. Jeff is told by the university that they will send the certificate to the Student Loan Company for him.

Some time after sending an application form for a loan, a lump sum arrives in his instant access account. After leaving a small portion of it in his current account to meet the costs of a small celebration, he transfers the rest of the money to the thirty-day notice higher interest account he already opened.

Patricia decides on a mortgage

Patricia is eager to buy her own place. After lengthy discussions with her bank manager father, she has decided to plump for an ordinary repayment mortgage. She is attracted by the simplicity of this type of mortgage. She was put off an endowment-linked mortgage by the stories she has heard that the returns on such policies might not be sufficient to meet the capital sum borrowed. She decides to obtain her mortgage from somewhere other than Greenbank as other lenders were offering cash incentives to new borrowers which Greenbank could not match.

John negotiates a reduction in interest rates

John, having been unable to move his business and personal accounts, has decided to leave his accounts where they are. He tells the branch manager that he is willing to offer them a second mortgage over his home and a personal guarantee of the business loan if they reduce the rate of interest and increase his overdraft limit. The bank agrees. John is careful to ensure his wife, who is joint owner of the home, obtains separate legal advice before she signs any documents guaranteeing the loans and mortgaging her interest in their home.

QUESTIONS AND ANSWERS

Q *My lender insists I take out credit insurance before making a loan. Can I avoid this cost?*

A If you already have insurance which covers loss of income, you may be able to persuade the lender to waive this particular condition of the loan. Otherwise, you will have to find a new lender. Of course, after the loan has been made, the lender cannot force you to take out such insurance unless the terms of the loan agreement expressly give him that ability.

Q *How long will it take for my loan application to be dealt with?*

A Applications can sometimes be dealt with very quickly, particularly where smaller sums are concerned. In this case the decision may be made almost immediately. Where larger loans are concerned, the procedure usually takes seven to fourteen days.

Q *If my endowment policy or unit trust investment is not sufficient to pay off my mortgage, what should I do?*

A You will remain liable for the amount outstanding on the loan after the insurance or unit trust proceeds have been applied in partial repayment. However, provided you had an otherwise good repayment record and the property is in good condition and has retained at least some value, you should be able to reschedule the loan. Effectively, you will be asking the mortgagee to extend the life of the loan by a few years.

DISCUSSION POINTS

1. What factors would you take into account in costing a loan?

2. What would you do if you found that you were unable to repay the loan?

3. How can you tie in your mortgage with plans for your retirement?

4
Making Credit Agreements

BUYING ON HIRE PURCHASE

Protecting yourself

There is one piece of legislation of which all people who enter into credit agreements, or pay for goods and services by way of a credit card, should be aware. The Consumer Credit Act 1974 (CCA 1974) is one of the most horrendously convoluted pieces of law ever enacted by Parliament. It is, however, very effective at protecting consumers. You don't need to attempt to read the Act, but bear in mind the following rights which it confers on you whenever you use a credit card, enter into HP or a personal loan agreement. To enable you to assert these rights, details of the relevant section numbers are given in the discussion which follows. The CCA 1974 applies to:

- all lending to individuals up to £15,000 but excluding overdrafts
- credit cards
- hire purchase and similar agreements.

Cooling off before buying
If you buy goods on credit, or incur credit by way of a personal loan and the agreement is one to which the Consumer Credit Act applies, you have the right under section 67 of the Act to cancel it within seven days of receiving a Notice of Cancellation. This Notice should be sent to your home shortly after you sign the credit agreement. It is a statutory requirement imposed on credit providers by the CCA 1974. This right is given to you to ensure that you have the ability to pull out of an agreement which you may have entered into either under pressure or in the heat of the moment. You do not have to explain why you are pulling out of the agreement. You do however, have to give back any goods or repay any money advanced. If you are to exercise this right you must do so within seven days of receiving the Notice.

Avoiding extortionate credit agreements
Under section 139 CCA 1974, anyone can apply to the court to have a credit agreement reopened and amended on the basis that the credit bargain was extortionate. A bargain is extortionate if the payments you have to make under it bear no relation to the value of the goods bought or original sum borrowed. Courts will only rewrite the agreement if the sums payable under it are especially exorbitant. They will not rewrite it if you have simply failed to find the cheapest source of finance.

Checking the terms of your agreement
As with all agreements where you take on financial obligations you must make sure that the agreements reflect the deal you believe you have entered into. The CCA 1974 compels those organisations providing credit to put all of the following matters on their standard form agreements in plain language:

- the amount of the credit given or the credit limit
- the time at which repayments must be made
- the amount of the repayments
- the APR
- the cash price, the total cost of the credit and the total sum you have to pay.

If some or all of these details are missing you can avoid the agreement.

Completing an HP agreement

Using goods as hirer
When you buy goods on HP terms you do not own those goods until you have paid all of the instalments due under the agreement, and then paid the final option price to acquire title to the goods themselves. Before that you are effectively using the goods as a hirer.

Giving goods back
If you do not pay the HP instalments on time the owner of them (the person you bought them from or, more commonly, the finance company) can repossess them. What happens if you miss the last payment and the owner tries to repossess? You may have paid most of the price but not acquired the title to the goods. The agreement will usually entitle you to a repayment of at least part of the

instalments paid by you already. If it does not, section 100 CCA 1974 gives you a statutory right to such a rebate. You would also be able to apply to the court for more time to pay in such a case. In any event, if you have paid more than one-third of the total due to the HP company, they cannot repossess the goods without first obtaining a court's permission. You would have the right to be represented at any hearing to ask for more time to pay.

Asserting rights against a finance company
If you bought goods on credit supplied by a finance company, and if the goods costs more than £100, the finance company is equally liable for any claim you have against the trader from whom you bought the goods. If the goods are not delivered or you did not get what you paid for, you may be able to claim from the credit or finance company.

USING A CREDIT CARD

Distinguishing between debit, charge and credit cards

Debit cards
This type of card does not involve taking out any credit at all and so does not fall within the scope of the CCA 1974. The two most popular cards in use are Switch and Delta. The cards are used as an alternative to writing a cheque. The purchase price paid with a debit card is taken from the current or other account in respect of which the card was issued. The seller swipes the card through an electronic funds transfer at the point of sale, or EFTPOS, machine and is advised if there are sufficient funds in the account.

Charge cards
American Express and Diners Club are the best known examples of charge cards. They are used to pay for goods and services and the user receives a statement each month. The cardholder should pay the sums outstanding in full each month. Interest will be charged on sums which are not paid when due and so there is an element of credit (albeit unauthorised) given with such cards. In order to obtain such a card you will have to pay both an initial enrolment fee and an annual membership fee. As discussed in Chapter 3, whatever the fee is called it should be taken into account when you are costing different methods of borrowing.

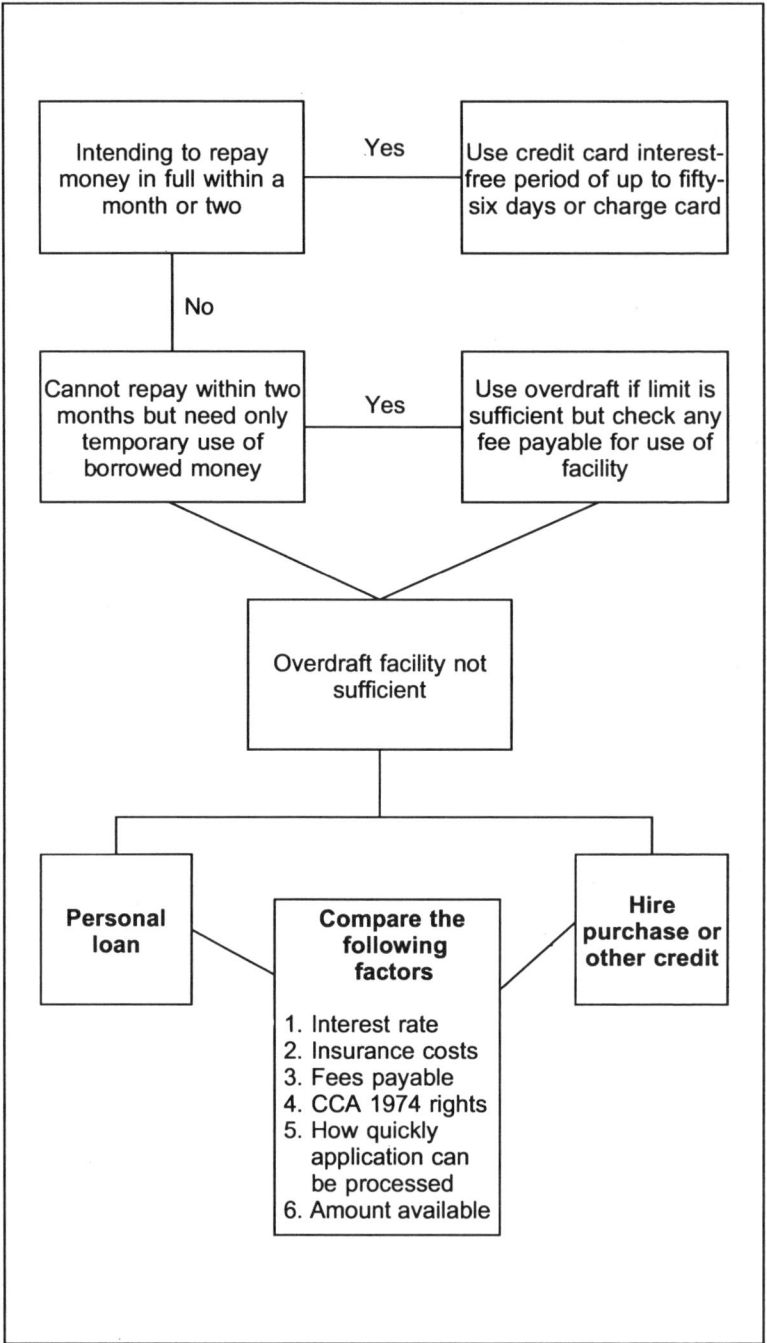

Fig. 5. Choosing the best credit option.

Credit cards

These cards are available from banks, building societies and numerous other organisations such as the bigger department stores. The card issuer gives the customer a card such as Visa or Mastercard and specifies the credit limit. The cardholder can buy goods or services up to that limit, using the card to pay. The cardholder receives a statement each month.

Unlike a charge card the user does not have to pay the full amount on the statement each month. The card issuer will specify a minimum amount each month which the cardholder has to pay, usually approximately 5 per cent of the total amount shown on the statement. Interest is charged on the balance outstanding from time to time. An annual fee may be payable to the card issuer and it may also require you to pay a small insurance premium each month as payment protection. See page 50.

Fifty-six days' free credit

Most credit card issuers only charge interest on balances which are outstanding twenty-five days after the due date for the next monthly payment. This means that, depending on the number of days in the calendar month, when you receive your statement and when you used the card, you can obtain free credit up to the limit on your card for fifty-six days.

Asserting rights against a credit card issuer

If you purchase goods or services with a credit card you usually acquire valuable rights against the card issuer. In particular, if the goods you bought using the card fail to be delivered, the company you bought the services from becomes insolvent (either bankrupt or in liquidation), or it simply does not perform as promised, you may require the card issuer to recredit your account with the amount of the purchase price. This applies if the goods or services cost more than £100.

MAKING LEASE AGREEMENTS

Leasing goods

Leases of goods (but not flats, houses or other property) fall within the scope of the CCA 1974. Consequently you have the rights outlined above, insofar as these apply to a situation where there is no sale of goods. Under a lease, also termed a chattel lease by some organisations, you do not acquire ownership of goods. Effectively

	LOAN OR OVERDRAFT	CREDIT CARD	CHARGE CARD	HIRE PURCHASE
Interest	Usually variable but fixed rate loans are available	Variable rate	Variable rate on sums not paid when due	Fixed and variable rates apply, check the agreement
Relative cost	Tends to be the cheapest form of borrowing	Initial interest-free period of up to fifty-six days. After this period interest rates and other fees make this form of credit more expensive than most overdrafts.	No interest payable if full payment is made each month. If not the interest rate will be at least as high as credit cards	No interest-free period usually, unless advertised as 0 per cent finance in which case look for other costs like insurance premiums and fees
Amounts available	Overdraft limit will depend on our income. Loan amount will depend on your ability to make interest payments on that sum	Credit limit determined by your income	Spending limit determined by your income	Amount of credit determined by the purchase price of the item
Requirement for security to be given	May be unsecured or secured by a charge or mortgage	Unsecured	Unsecured	Unsecured
Lender's rights	To sue for repayment of the sum borrowed if not repaid on the due date. If security given the lender may sell the asset over which it has a charge	To sue for the outstanding amount	To sue for the outstanding amount	To sue for the balance of the amount outstanding. To repossess goods (only with a court order if one-third paid)
Your rights	To have cheques met when there are no funds in your account but you remain within the overdraft limit. To have the sum advanced on loan paid to you	To use the card to pay for goods and services up to the credit limit specified, until the card issuer informs you to stop using it	To use the card to pay for goods and services up to the agreed spending limit, until the card issuer informs you to stop using it	To use the goods as hirer whilst paying the HP instalments. To acquire ownership of the goods for a nominal sum at the end of the hire period. To retain the goods until a court order is obtained, allowing the finance company to repossess where you have paid one third of the price already
Application of CCA 1974	Yes, if the lending is to an individual and is for a sum less than £15,000	Yes	No	Yes

Fig. 6. Analysing the credit options.

you are paying to have the use of someone else's goods for the period of the lease.

CREDIT REFERENCE AGENCIES

Checking your creditworthiness
Whenever you apply for a loan, or purchase something on credit, the lender has to satisfy itself that you will meet the repayments due under the agreement. One of the commonest ways they can obtain some information about your credit history is to ask a credit reference agency to give it a report on you.

What is contained in a credit reference
The report will contain information on:

- any loan you have taken out
- any credit card you may have
- any other credit agreements you have entered into, including those which are now completely repaid
- any mortgage you may have outstanding
- any court judgements which have been made against you
- details of any banking accounts you have opened.

These details will be on various computers around the country to which the credit reference agencies have access.

Using your rights under the Data Protection Act
It can be very worrying if you are refused credit due to an unfavourable report by a credit reference agency. You can ask for a copy of any data kept about you on computer. The Data Protection Act gives you the right to obtain a copy of the relevant entries on payment of a small fee, currently £10. Write to the person who refused you credit, requesting a copy of the entries it has on its computers. If it replies that the credit reference was obtained from a third party, follow the paper trail by getting that party's details and writing to them. If you are having trouble obtaining copies you can contact the Data Protection Registrar, whose details are given in Useful Addresses. They will help you and provide you with a booklet explaining your rights in detail.

CASE STUDIES

Jeff cools off

Jeff goes to a store and buys a new hi-fi system. He wants to cheer himself up after a long term of hard work. He signs an agreement to pay for the system on hire purchase terms. The shop checks his details over the telephone with his bank and a credit reference agency, and are happy to make the sale.

When he gets home later that day Jeff realises he has spent too much money on the system and is worried about keeping up the payments. He thinks about it for a few days. During the next week a further copy of the HP agreement arrives at his flat along with a Notice of Cancellation. This tells him that he has the right to cancel the agreement on returning the goods if he wants to. He has seven days to make up his mind. He decides to return the goods and cancel the agreement.

Patricia nearly goes on holiday

Patricia and a group of friends decide to buy a cheap holiday, booking at the last possible moment in order to get the best deal. The next week the group learns that the tour operator has gone into liquidation. Patricia has paid for the holiday on her credit card. When she hears the news she telephones the card issuer and asks them what she should do. They tell her that they will refund her money, save for a small excess amount, because under the CCA 1974 they are equally liable with the tour operator to make sure she gets what she paid for. Based on their assurance the group re-books their holiday with another operator, being careful to make sure they pay with their credit cards.

John runs up a credit card bill

John has exceeded the limits on both his overdraft and business loans for his company. The company has to pay a key supplier or it will lose a major piece of business. He decides to draw cash on his credit card. Like most cards he can both use it in ATM machines and draw cash over the counter at banks and building societies. When he reads his next statement he finds that he has been paying interest on the large cash sum he drew right from the day he got the cash. When he looks closely at the terms and conditions under which the card was issued he sees that for cash advances on the card there is no free credit period at all. Drawing cash on a credit card is not as cheap a way to borrow even short-term money as he had thought.

QUESTIONS AND ANSWERS

Q *Is it dearer buying goods with a credit card?*

A No. The price of goods and services should be the same whether you pay cash or use your credit card in almost all shops in this country. Practices differ in some other countries where it is wise to check whether any additional price is payable. The reason some shops may ask for a higher price is that they pay a commission to the credit card company of about 5 per cent. They will want to cover this charge.

Q *How do I know whether someone will accept payment by credit card?*

A Retailers display stickers in their shops which indicate which debit, charge and credit cards they will accept.

Q *I have lost my copy of the credit agreement. How do I get another copy?*

A Under the CCA 1974 (section 77) you can obtain a further copy of any credit agreement from the person or organisation which has provided the credit, for a fee of 50p. They should send a copy to you within twelve working days of receiving your request. They cannot take any enforcement action against you under the agreement prior to letting you have a copy so you can check the terms.

DISCUSSION POINTS

1. Why would it be wise to use a credit card to pay for valuable items which you buy and which are being sent to you through the post?

2. What factors would influence your decision to buy goods on credit?

3. What are the advantages of a debit card?

5
Banking On-Line

MAKING A TRANSFER OF MONEY

Using the BACS system

The **Bankers Automated Clearing System (BACS)** is one of the commonest ways employers make transfers to pay their employees' wages. It is a paperless transaction in that the employer does not have to issue any cheques. Everything is done by computers. The whole process takes three days.

- On the first day the person who wishes to make the transfer supplies the details of the payments to be made to the processing unit of BACS.

- On the second day BACS processes these details to make sure all the banks concerned have the necessary details to make appropriate entries in the accounts of their customers.

- On the third day the transferor's bank will debit its account and the bank of each individual receiving a payment will credit the appropriate account.

Everything is done by the BACS computer system.

A similar process applies to transfer instructions given by one individual to pay money by transfer into the account of another. Once an instruction to make a transfer has been given you only have a very short time in which to stop the transaction going through. You must stop it before the close of the second day.

Giving a transfer instruction
It is possible to initiate the transfer process by telephoning your bank with an instruction and giving them the relevant details. However, most organisations will insist on a written confirmation before the end of the first day of the process in order to complete the

```
┌─────────────────────────────────────────────────────────────────┐
│                        ┌──────────────────┐                       │
│                        │    CUSTOMER      │                       │
│    Instruction in      │    MAKING        │                       │
│    writing given to    │    TRANSFER      │                       │
│    debit transferor's  └──────────────────┘                       │
│    account                                                        │
│                        Paying bank                                │
│    ┌────────────────┐  advises        ┌──────────────────┐        │
│    │ PAYING BANK    │  recipient's bank│ RECEIVING BANK   │        │
│    │ TRANSFERS      │  of sum to be    │ CREDITS          │        │
│    │ FUNDS TO       │  credited to their│ RECIPIENT'S      │        │
│    │ RECIPIENT'S BANK│ customer's      │ ACCOUNT          │        │
│    └────────────────┘  account         └──────────────────┘        │
│                                        Recipient bank             │
│    ┌────────────────┐                  does not                   │
│    │ RECIPIENT      │                  normally inform            │
│    │ RECEIVES MONEY │                  their customer             │
│    │ IN ITS ACCOUNT │                  of the funds               │
│    │ AFTER MAXIMUM  │                  arrival unless             │
│    │ OF THREE DAYS, │                  asked to do so             │
│    │ USUALLY SOONER │                                             │
│    └────────────────┘                                             │
└─────────────────────────────────────────────────────────────────┘
```

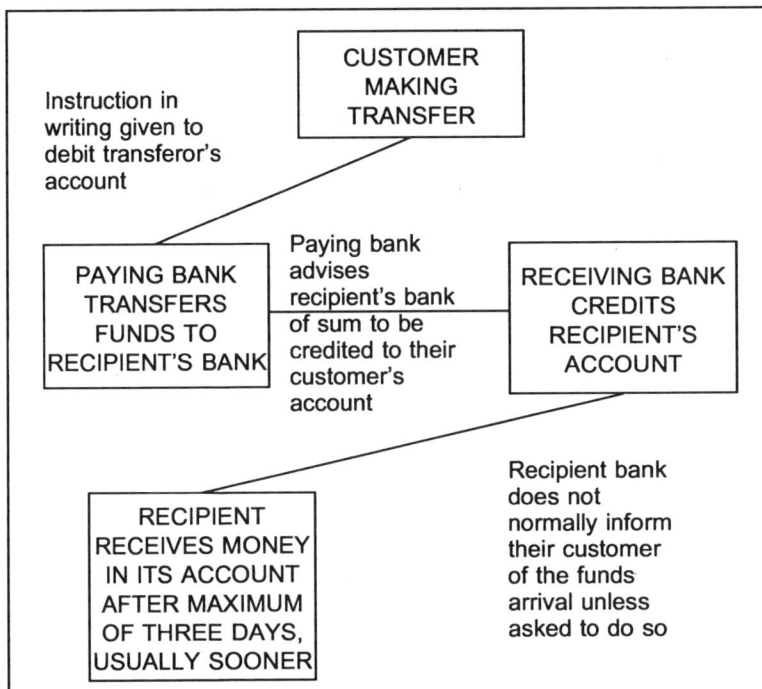

Fig. 7. Typical sequence of events for an electronic transfer of money.

transfer. If you fill in a bank giro slip this can be processed in the manner described above.

Paying for a transfer
A fee will be charged for making a transfer and consequently they tend to be cost effective only in cases of great urgency or where the amounts involved are large. Some organisations impose a minimum amount which is the smallest that can be moved in this manner. With the advent of telephone and computer banking such limitations are likely to become less common.

TELEPHONE BANKING SERVICES

Dealing on the telephone
A primary concern whenever business is transacted over the telephone is security. For this reason most organisations which provide this facility will give you a **Personal Identity Number** (a **PIN**

is similar to one you receive with an ATM card) or some other form of security code word to authorise transactions on the telephone. It is important that you keep this code confidential, as it could be used by any third party to gain access to your details and move money out of your account.

Paying bills by telephone

Most banks and building societies will allow you to transact the following over the telephone without charging you extra:

- transferring money to another account
- obtaining details of recent transactions on your account
- obtaining your account balance
- authorising small loans or overdrafts
- obtaining details of advisory services offered by the organisation
- obtaining details of mortgages and other services
- paying bills.

You may have to pay the costs of the telephone call but usually this is charged at local rates if it is not a freephone number.

USING SMARTCARDS

One of the most recent developments in retail banking is the introduction of so-called smartcards. These are not yet widely available but should become quite common within the next year or so.

What is a smartcard?

A smartcard is essentially a mini computer. It is a plastic card which looks very similar to any credit, charge or debit card. It even has a piece of magnetic tape on the back like these other cards. However, on ordinary cards the magnetic tape contains only very limited amounts of information. When a seller swipes the card through an EFTPOS machine when you make a purchase, the card sends a signal down a telephone line to a central computer which tells him whether you have the funds to make the purchase, or a sufficiently large credit limit and so on. All of this can take some time to complete.

A smartcard has a microprocessor built into it which can hold many more details of your account, any credit limit and any previous purchases which might have used up part of your credit limit in whole or in part. It can also hold much more sophisticated information, allowing third parties to identify you. The basic idea is that when the smartcard is swiped through a till it will be read immediately without having to send a signal down a telephone line to a central computer. Thus it will save you and the shopkeeper time.

Filling up with money
It is hoped that banks, building societies and other organisations will be able to issue cards credited with specific amounts of money. These can then be used up as a number of transactions are completed over time. They will be capable of being used at retailers and at cash machines.

USING A CASH MACHINE

Having a cash card
To be able to use automatic teller machines (ATMs) you will need to apply for a cash card. These are usually freely available whenever you open an account. You will be given a PIN which you have to key into a machine. This gives you access to the various services available through these machines which will include one or more of the following:

- obtaining cash
- paying in cheques
- paying bills
- receiving mini statements
- ordering new cheque and paying-in books
- making transfers between accounts.

Keeping your PIN secure
In Chapter 8, which deals with complaining to your bank, you will see that one of the commonest complaints concerns unauthorised withdrawals from accounts via an ATM machine. The organisations which operate ATMs have argued more or less consistently that the system they use to track movements on accounts via ATMs are infallible. One of the reasons they have been able to do this is that it very often turns out that such phantom withdrawals are in fact occasioned by unauthorised use of an ATM card by someone who has obtained the card and the PIN. In most cases the use is by other family members!

Paying for the use of ATMs
If you use an ATM operated by someone other than the

organisation which issued you with the cash card, make sure that you are not being charged a fee each time you use the card in that machine. See page 23.

BANKING ON COMPUTERS

Using a computer bank account

A number of banks and building societies are introducing fully computerised banking services. These are available to people who have a computer link in their home (businesses have had such links for a while) and a modem to allow them to link their computer to the outside world via a telephone link. In some cases it is necessary to connect to one of the Internet service providers such as Compuserve, AOL or the Microsoft Network before you can take advantage of the facilities offered through the computer banking service. Connecting to the Internet through a service provider will cost about £10–15 per month depending on how frequently you use the service.

The advantages of these links are:

• You are able to call up full details of transactions on your account at home.

• The facility is available 365 days a year and 24 hours a day.

• You can download a statement into a money management software program such as Microsoft's Money or Quicken's Finance software if you have them.

• You can discuss issues which arise on your account by e-mail.

• Some banks will deal with loan and overdraft applications on-line and give an immediate response.

Obtaining the right software
In order to access these services you will need to load the organisation's customised software onto your computer. The software is usually made available free of charge at any branch, or may be found at the World Wide Web site and downloaded from there.

Making transactions secure

One of the biggest issues concerning on-line banking is security.

There have been well publicised cases where computer experts have 'hacked' into supposedly secure telephone lines and obtained details from computers which they have then used for their own financial gain. Recently, the methods available to financial organisations to encode data which has to be sent along telephone lines has become much more sophisticated. This so-called encryption software can now protect data from all but the most expert computer hackers.

And there is the rub. As soon as the encryption software armour becomes more complicated, the people who would use any information for their own nefarious purposes develop more techniques to pierce it. All that can be said with any certainty at the moment is that there is a very small risk of your details being used by a third party in an unauthorised manner. In my opinion the risk is probably smaller than somebody getting hold of your credit card details for unauthorised use when you fill in the details of an order form which you then send through the post.

SHOPPING ON-LINE

Anyone who is connected to the Internet may go shopping in the comfort of their own home, at any hour of the day or night. Numerous shopping sites on the World Wide Web offer goods for sale. The usual method of payment is by credit card. What has been said already about security and encryption in relation to computerised banking services is equally relevant in this context.

Tips for virtual shoppers

- Always check that your credit card details are being sent over a 'secure line'.

- Never give your credit card details to anyone who pops up on e-mail, especially in so-called 'chat rooms' or newsgroups, and asks for them.

- Only use the forms available at the site from which you are buying.

- If the site you are buying goods from is outside the country in which you live, you may be paying in a different currency. Any adverse movement in the exchange rate between the time of purchase and the date your card issuer sends you a statement will be for you to pay.

- Always keep a written record of purchases.

- Telephone the organisation if the goods do not arrive within the stated delivery period.

- If there are no contact addresses, telephone numbers and fax details do not bother buying as e-mail accounts have a habit of disappearing quickly.

- Read the sections in Chapter 4 which deal with your rights to a refund from a credit card company.

CASE STUDIES

Jeff makes a money transfer

Jeff has a friend who is holidaying in Greece. He is telephoned late one night by his friend who has lost all his money, travellers' cheques and cards. He asks Jeff to send some money and gives him his address in Greece. Next morning Jeff calls Western Union on their freephone number (details in Useful Addresses) and they tell him he can send a **moneygram** to one of their offices in a town very close to where his friend is staying. He reads over his credit card details and they effect the transfer straight away. He is charged a small fee for the service.

Patricia buys a book

Patricia is surfing the Internet when she comes across details of a book she wants to buy. She completes the electronic order form and checks that she is sending the details over a secure connection before pressing the send button. The shop is in the United States and she has checked the exchange rate so she knows within a few pennies what the cost should be when she receives her card statement, assuming no great movements in the exchange rate occur. Her card issuer provides her with a remedy if the book does not turn up and the goods bought with the card are automatically covered by insurance for the first ninety days.

John stops a money transfer

John issued an instruction to his bank to telegraphically transfer £20,000 to an investment company in the Cayman Islands two days ago. When he picks up the morning newspaper he sees that the company concerned is being investigated by the Serious Fraud Office. He immediately phones his account manager to try and stop the transfer. The bank tells him that he is lucky. Normally he would have been too late. However, because of the time difference between the Cayman Islands and the United Kingdom the bank has not yet fully processed the transfer and can stop it.

QUESTIONS AND ANSWERS

Q   *My wages have not been paid into my account as usual. Can I claim against my bank?*

A   Probably not. Only if the bank has been negligent in some way would you be able to mount a claim. Even then it would only be for any extra costs you incurred in borrowing money to tide you over until your account was credited. Unless you can prove greater damage occurred, directly as a result of their negligence, your claim will be limited.

Q   *Are ATMs perfect?*

A   This is the cause of much heated argument between customers and financial organisations. The only thing which can be said with any certainty is that it will be difficult to prove that any loss you have suffered is from a defect in a bank's computer systems, rather than someone getting hold of your card details and PIN. Banks tend to defend such cases very strenuously because of the impact on their customers' confidence should their computer systems be shown to be at fault.

Q   *How long does it take for a debit card transaction to show up on my statement?*

A   Around three days, although as the banks improve their technology this period will gradually become smaller until eventually all entries on your account will happen immediately.

DISCUSSION POINTS

1.   What concerns would you have about using a computer link for banking transactions?

2.   How would you protect yourself when buying goods over the Internet?

3.   Do you think smartcards will replace cheques and cash?

6
Obtaining Advice on
Financial Services

PLANNING FOR THE FUTURE

Saving for retirement

Chapter 1 discussed how to assess your wealth and how much you may be able to save. This part of the book looks at some of the more popular financial products which are on the market and how to obtain advice on them. For anyone who wishes to go into this subject in more detail, *Managing Your Personal Finances* by John Claxton, another book in this series, may also be very useful. The key points to planning savings for your future are:

- Work hard at obtaining as much information as you can.

- Take your time in assessing that information.

- Talk to financial planning professionals after you have digested the information and sorted out your own financial position.

- Always ask for a full explanation of anything you do not understand.

- Do not be pushed into spending money, for that is what you are doing, buying security for later, if you do not know how something works.

Spreading risk

Any investment portfolio should contain a range of investments which balance higher and lower risk products. The aim of any strategy is to optimise the amount of return, but not by putting all of the sums invested at severe risk of their value being eroded. What exactly do people mean by low, medium and high risk?

Low risk
Low risk investments are those saving and investment products

which do not put the capital amount at any risk of melting away should the particular investment prove to be less successful than hoped. An important part of a low risk investment is the financial strength of the institution which handles the money. The large commercial banks, building societies and insurance companies are regarded as safe in this respect because such institutions seldom fail (eg, by going into liquidation) and when they do there is a protection scheme which provides a safety net for their clients.

Medium risk
Medium risk investments are those which may put any capital invested at risk, but which spread the risk that the value of the capital will diminish by investing it in a number of sources which, when taken together, have only a small chance of not increasing in value overall. The institution handling the funds will usually have a proven track record of investment success and financial safety.

High risk
High risk investments are typically those in which the amount of capital invested could be lost in whole or in part if the investment does not perform as well as is hoped. The institution handling the funds may not have a proven track record. It is more likely that the sum you invest will be used by the organisation to buy shares (or in some cases units in unit trusts) in start-up companies, companies in 'growing' or 'emerging' economies elsewhere in the world, or otherwise concentrated in funds or shares which expect you to pay for the higher returns offered by putting your capital at significant risk of loss of value.

The following examples will give you some idea of how some of the more popular financial products, described in more detail below, could be ranked in the context of risk to capital.

Low risk	Medium risk	High risk
Bank accounts	Unit trusts	Shares
Building society accounts	Income or distribution bonds	Specialist unit trusts
Endowment policies		Commodities

Knowing the risks
A final word on risk. As anyone who had money invested in The Bank of Credit and Commerce International (known better as BCCI) will already know, even large financial companies go under.

When you make an investment, part of your risk assessment should take into account the presence or absence of any protection scheme should the company fail. The small print in a document which states that the value of an investment may go up or down is there for a good reason. It is to ensure you have no claim against the company if your investment fails to produce the returns you had hoped to obtain.

Risk assessment is your task. Explaining what the risk might be is the job of the relevant bank, building society or investment house.

POPULAR FINANCIAL PRODUCTS

Building a fund to buy an annuity

Providing a retirement income
One method of providing a stable income for retirement is to purchase an **annuity**. This means that you pay a lump sum to a company (the annuity provider) and in return they will pay you an annual income of a specific amount (which can be paid to you in monthly instalments) for the rest of your life.

Buying an annuity
The current cost of purchasing annuities is approximately 9 per cent. This is called the **annuity rate**. In broad terms this means that at retirement you would have to pay a company a lump sum of £100,000 in order to buy an annual income of £9,000 for the rest of your life. The annuity rate changes from time to time so the amount of steady income your money can buy consequently depends upon the prevailing annuity rate at the time of purchase. You may be able to ensure that upon your death some lesser percentage of the annual income is paid by the annuity provider to your husband or wife who survives you. Building a fund to buy an annuity later is one of the main reasons people invest in some of the financial products described below.

Investing in with-profits endowment insurance

Paying premiums
This is one of the most well known and popular methods of saving

for retirement. You pay a monthly or annual premium to an insurer who invests that money for you. In return the company agrees to pay you a specific sum called the 'basic sum assured' when the policy matures. Additional sums are added to the basic sum assured over the life of the policy. Each year you receive a statement telling you how much has been added to your investment.

Receiving bonuses
So-called bonuses are added to your investment – the basic sum assured. During the lifetime of the policy reversionary bonuses are paid every year at a certain percentage (higher or lower depending on the health of the economy) and these then form a guaranteed part of your returns.

A terminal bonus is also payable when the policy matures (that is, when the insurance company is obliged to repay your investment with all its returns earned), either at the date fixed for maturity at the outset or possibly upon death. Terminal bonuses have historically been quite large, but they are never guaranteed by insurance companies which have complete discretion over whether to pay them or not. The fact is that the level of terminal bonus is crucial to the overall success of the investment and there is market pressure for insurance companies to make these bonuses as high as they can.

Investing in personal pension plans

Benefiting from company pension schemes
The basic rule is that if your employer runs a company pension scheme it is almost always sensible to join it. Employers cover the administration costs of the scheme and will make contributions to it on your behalf. There are two types of scheme.

- In a **money purchase scheme** (sometimes called 'defined contribution schemes') both you and the employer make contributions to a fund which is then invested. At retirement you are allocated part of the fund. You can take part as a lump sum and/or use part to buy an annuity.

- In a **final salary scheme** (sometimes called a 'defined benefit scheme') the amount of your pension depends on your salary at the date you retire. Using a formula which takes into account this and your time with the company, a level of payment is calculated. You will need to ask your employer how the payments are calculated if you are in such a scheme as all schemes are different.

Setting up your own personal pension plan
People pay into their own **personal pension plan** for a number of reasons. They may wish to top up any benefit from a company scheme if they have moved jobs or they may be self-employed. The basic procedure is as follows:

* Periodic payments are made to a pension provider. These can be annual, monthly or at irregular intervals.

* The pension provider invests the funds in a spread of low, medium and sometimes higher risk investments. You may be asked to specify what percentage of the sum you pay goes into investments in each of these risk categories.

* A fund is built up over time. The later your retirement age, the bigger the fund.

* You specify a retirement age which can be at any time from 50 to 75.

* At the specific retirement age you can opt to receive a lump sum or use it to buy an annuity (or a mixture of the two).

Getting the tax man to contribute
One of the benefits of a personal pension plan is that for every £100 paid in, you pay £75 and the tax man pays £25, assuming you are a basic rate taxpayer. For those who pay tax at the higher rate, provided details of the contributions made are on your tax return, additional tax relief can be claimed. There are limits on the amount of contributions you can make and still claim tax relief. For people age 35 and under a maximum sum of 17.5 per cent of earnings can be used to make such contributions. The percentage of earnings which can be used then increases.

Age	Usable percentage of earnings
36–45	20
46–50	25
51–55	30
56–60	35
61 and over	40

When you take out a personal pension plan, ask the company to let you have the forms you need to claim tax relief.

Investing in Personal Equity Plans

Personal Equity Plans, or **PEPs**, are a relatively new way to invest money to obtain tax-free returns. They are sold by most building societies, banks and insurance companies. You may invest up to £6,000 in any one tax year, either in one lump sum or on a monthly basis. This is invested by the company in unit trusts or shares. Units in unit trusts are simply a collective investment in a wide variety of stocks and shares, held in one bundle. This allows the trust to spread risk effectively. Any income received or capital gains made on the investment in your PEP is free of tax. PEPs are designed to be attractive to tax payers who can afford to tie up their money for five years or more. They are medium-risk as the value of the units can fall and so erode the initial capital invested.

Investing in TESSA

TESSA stands for **Tax Exempt Special Savings Account**. You can open a TESSA in the same way as any bank or other savings account. Saving is by monthly payments into the account or payment of a lump sum. You can invest between £5,000 and £9,000 in a TESSA.

The main benefit of a TESSA is that the interest you earn on the account is entirely free of income tax, provided you comply with the terms and conditions under which the account is held. There are restrictions on the amount which you can withdraw from the account without causing it to lose its tax exempt status. The most you can withdraw is a sum equal to the amount of interest actually earned on the account, less the amount of tax at the basic rate which would have been paid on that amount but for the tax exempt status.

TESSAs are offered for fixed periods (usually five years) and may carry a fixed or variable rate of interest on the sum invested. Interest is credited to the account at fixed periods during the life of the account. They are low-risk investments.

Investing in bonds

Finding the right bond for you
The number of types of **bonds** in which you may invest is enormous. An investment in bonds can be anything from a high-risk specialist investment in bonds issued by companies which wish to borrow money through an issue of debt-related bonds on the stock market, to a low-risk investment with your high street bank. The former is like investing in quoted shares, the latter akin to having a deposit savings

account with a bank or building society. When you are considering investing in a bond, pay particular attention to the terms on which it is issued. Ask if you run the risk of your capital losing value.

Using income or distribution bonds
These are the questions you should ask if you are considering an investment in a bond.

- Can I lose the whole or some part of my capital?

- Is there a fixed rate of interest or is this variable?

- Can I withdraw the interest earned at any time?

- Are there any restrictions on withdrawing amounts of capital from the account?

- If I withdraw any sums from the account, do I have to pay any penalties?

- What are the initial charges for investing and are there any annual management fees?

Going offshore
Most bonds are long-term investments designed for those who can afford to tie up their money for periods of five years or more. Some companies offer higher rates of interest than others because they invest the money offshore, that is, beyond the reach of the tax man. Make sure that when you receive your payment at the end of the investment you know how much tax, if any, you will have to pay. When money is being sent offshore it pays to do some homework on the company which has custody of the cash. Investing with the offshore arm of a high street bank is low-risk. Investing with a company which has no tangible connection with the country in which you live means taking a rather higher level of risk.

CHOOSING A FINANCIAL ADVISER

Obtaining information

Asking friends and family
One of the best sources of information on financial advisers is friends and family. There can be no better guide than satisfaction of

people you know with the services provided. Remember to compare like with like. A good insurance adviser may not know much about investment bonds. A good banker might not know much about endowment policies.

Using newspapers and magazines
The broadsheet newspapers all have columns which offer financial advice on a whole host of matters. These sections usually also carry advertisements from companies which will enable you to obtain free information or even a free personal financial review. If you feel uneasy about having someone call on you at home, make it clear you wish to deal with them in writing initially. Never be rushed into an investment.

There are several monthly magazines which deal with all aspects of financial planning. Browsing through the pages of these journals will give you more than enough contact details.

Understanding the two types of adviser
There are two types of financial adviser. The first type is the 'tied' adviser who is employed by a company to sell just their products. This type of adviser can only advise you on the products offered by that one company. He cannot give you advice on whether any other type of product sold by another organisation would be a better investment for your particular circumstances.

The second type of adviser is the independent adviser who, as the name suggests, is not employed by any one financial services company and can give advice on any organisation's financial products.

Signing a client agreement
Whoever your adviser is, you should be asked to sign a **client agreement** which sets out the basis upon which the advice is given. Be sure that this makes clear the price for the advice. Most companies of any size offer free advice, at least initially. The agreement will usually state that you are responsible for the accuracy of the financial information on which the advice is based. It is sensible to be slightly pessimistic when assessing the amount of disposable income you might have available for these purposes!

INSTRUCTING AN ADVISER

It is important that your financial adviser knows:

Anytown Insurance Co Limited
Insurance House
Anytown Court
Anytown
Anycounty
AA2 BB2

Our Client
Address   Date

Regulator's Statement
Those who advise on life assurance, pensions or unit trust products are:

EITHER: representatives of one company
OR: independent advisers

YOUR ADVISER REPRESENTS THE ANYTOWN INSURANCE CO LIMITED AND ACTS ON ITS BEHALF. YOUR ADVISER CAN ONLY GIVE YOU ADVICE ON THE LIFE ASSURANCE, PENSIONS AND UNIT TRUST PRODUCTS OF ANYTOWN INSURANCE CO LIMITED. BECAUSE YOUR ADVISER IS NOT INDEPENDENT HE OR SHE CANNOT ADVISE YOU ON PRODUCTS OF THIS TYPE AVAILABLE FROM COMPANIES OTHER THAN ANYTOWN INSURANCE CO LIMITED.

Anytown Insurance Co Limited undertake that the initial advisory service provided by them will be without obligation on your part and shall be free of charge. You undertake to provide Anytown Insurance with all details and documents specific to your financial position and requirements in order for them to draw up a Financial Plan. You understand that if the information you have provided is in any way inaccurate or incomplete it may affect the accuracy and the value of the Financial Plan and any other advice given to you by Anytown Insurance.

Subject only to the above Anytown takes responsibility for any advice given to you by any of its representatives.

You may inspect any documents including data stored on computer relating to your dealings with Anytown Insurance. These will be held for a period of six years.

The product range of Anytown Insurance includes all those types of products listed on the attached schedule.

ANYTOWN INSURANCE CO LIMITED IS REGULATED IN THE CONDUCT OF INVESTMENT BUSINESS BY THE SECURITIES AND INVESTMENT BOARD AND IS BOUND BY ITS RULES. ANYTOWN INSURANCE CO LIMITED HAS AGREED TO PUT INTO PRACTICE THE ASSOCIATION OF BRITISH INSURERS' CODE OF PRACTICE FOR SELLING GENERAL INSURANCE.

IF YOU SHOULD HAVE A COMPLAINT ABOUT THE SERVICES OR PRODUCTS PROVIDED BY ANYTOWN INSURANCE PLEASE WRITE TO THE CUSTOMER SERVICES MANAGER AT THE ABOVE ADDRESS OR TELEPHONE 0181 444 2222 FAX 0181 444 3333.

Please sign and retain one copy of this document as it may be important in any later dealings you have with Anytown Insurance.

Signed by..............

Date..............

Fig. 8. A client agreement with a financial adviser.

- The amount of your income and outgoings so that he can determine how much you can reasonably afford to spend on providing for your retirement.

- The details of any capital you have, such as the amount of any equity in your house if you own it subject to a mortgage.

- Details of the value of any pension fund into which you have already paid contributions.

- The details of any insurance you already hold.

- The category of risk you are willing to take with the money you invest. Usually he will ask you to split the sums you are to invest between low, medium and higher risk investment.

- How much you would like to have available for your retirement.

The last piece of information needs some careful thought. Ask yourself what expenses you will have on retirement – will the mortgage be paid? – and what you want to do – travel or buy a place in the country? It will become clear that you will need to spend some time working out your objectives.

Keeping records
Always keep receipts for contributions, statements on how your investment is doing and policy documents in a safe place. You may need to produce these for tax purposes. Most companies will issue an original policy document and a copy. Keep the original in a fireproof drawer or safety box. You might like to keep such documents with your will.

CASE STUDIES

Jeff receives a surprise
Jeff has not been planning on making any longer-term savings. However, he receives a lump sum from a with-profits endowment policy taken out for his benefit by his parents when he was younger. He decides that he will not put it into a TESSA or PEP, because he does not yet have any taxable income and so does not benefit as much from tax exempt savings as would a tax payer. He decides to reinvest the sum in unit trusts. He believes these are lower-risk than

investing directly in shares, yet will allow him to share in the potentially greater returns from investing in quoted shares.

Patricia meets TESSA

Patricia decides she would benefit from investing in something which is relatively safe and yet produces a slightly higher return than the normal savings accounts. As a tax payer, the additional income she will receive by not having to pay tax on interest earned from sums deposited in a TESSA fits the bill perfectly. She likes the flexibility of being able to make some withdrawals from the TESSA without losing the higher rate of return resulting from its tax exempt status.

John plans a pension

John has been paying into a personal pension plan for the last five years or so. He started the plan by transferring the benefits accrued in his company pension scheme when he left the job to set up his own business. He has been worried that his contributions have been too small to build up a big enough fund to buy the level of annuity he wanted on retirement. Now he is 40 he decides to increase his contributions to take account of the increased tax relief to which he is entitled. He also takes out an additional with-profits endowment policy to top up his fund and spread risk.

QUESTIONS AND ANSWERS

Q *When should I start paying for a pension?*

A The earlier you start, the better off you should be when you retire. As a general rule, if you are planning to retire at 65 you should be making contributions to a pension plan from 25 – 30 onwards.

Q *What would a typical savings portfolio consist of?*

A There is no such thing as a 'typical' savings portfolio, as each person will have a different view of the risks they are prepared to take and the amount they will need to achieve whatever plans they have made for retirement.

Q *If I change job, can I transfer my pension benefits to my new employer?*

A If your new employer has a similar pension scheme, you will be able to transfer the full value of your existing scheme benefits to the new one. If the new employer does not have a similar scheme, or has no company pension plan for you to join (some employers only allow you to join a scheme after you have worked for them for a certain number of years), you can transfer the benefits to a personal pension plan. Of course, another option is to leave your benefits in the old scheme and receive whatever benefits are due to you from that when you reach retirement age.

DISCUSSION POINTS

1. What are the three most important things you want to do on retirement and how much will they cost at present day rates?

2. Are you making the most of the tax benefits available to you in your current saving plan?

3. What risk are you prepared to take to obtain a higher return on your savings?

7
Business Banking

CHOOSING THE RIGHT LENDER

Using business centres

Many banks have special branches designated as business centres. They are staffed by people who have experience of providing finance to all kinds of businesses, large and small. These branches act as advisory centres for the bank's business customers who want to open accounts and arrange loans. If you are just starting out in business it is worthwhile contacting such branches in your area as they can provide valuable guidance.

Combining personal and business accounts

Remember that if you hold personal accounts with a different organisation from the one with which you propose setting up business accounts, they may suggest that those accounts should be transferred so that all of your banking is through the one organisation. Sometimes when you ask for a loan, it is a condition of granting the loan that a transfer of your personal accounts is made, particularly when you are asked to give a personal guarantee for the loan (see page 99). The reason a lender may ask for this is to give it the ability to set off any monies in your personal account against any liability you may have to the lender under the guarantee. The lender can only operate this set-off if your personal accounts are held at one of its own branches.

Making the right choice

All of the factors which were discussed in Chapter 1 in relation to personal banking services will be just as important in the context of opening a business account. However, it is vitally important that you feel confident that the people you will be dealing with where your business banks understand how your business operates.

For example, if your business is a hotel which depends on tourist levels, it may have greater income in the summer months. In the winter expenditure might be in excess of income, as accommodation levels drop and repairs and refurbishment have to be paid for. You need to ensure that your bank understands that the amount of your business overdraft will fluctuate during the year. The last thing you would need is a worried banker demanding repayment of all your outstanding loans just at the time builders are waiting to be paid for work!

Checking terms and conditions

Opening a business account is like any other business contract. Check what the terms on which you are doing business actually mean. The Banking Code of Best Practice states that banks should use plain language in their agreements. However, these agreements are sometimes written in technical language which is difficult for the uninitiated to understand. The best time to ask questions about points you do not understand is before the account is opened, as it may not be possible to rectify misunderstandings later.

APPLYING FOR BUSINESS LOANS

Choosing the right type of loan

Using an overdraft facility

Overdrafts are the most popular forms of borrowing, both for businesses and individuals. An organisation allows its customer to withdraw monies up to a specified limit even if the account is not in credit. There is, however, one very important distinction to be made between a loan and an overdraft facility.

> **An overdraft is repayable upon demand and the lender may make a demand at any time without giving any reason if it wishes, though most do give reasons.**

It is because of this that many businesses want the greater certainty of a business loan, rather than relying solely on an overdraft.

Checking important terms

The important terms to check with this type of facility are:

- the interest rate
- the period during which the facility will be available for use, commonly twelve months.

Using a loan facility
A loan may be for any period but is usually for two to five years. There will normally be a **loan agreement** drawn up between you and the lender which will set out the important terms governing the loan.

The most important difference between a loan and an overdraft is that the lender can only demand repayment of the loan in certain circumstances which must be set out in the loan agreement.

Another difference is that the lender may specify the purpose for which it is lending the money, for example to build a new shop, and in this case the money must only be used for that purpose and no other. Repayments of both capital and interest will have to be made periodically during the life of the loan.

Checking important terms
The important terms to check in this type of facility are:

- the amount of the loan

- the interest rate payable and how this may vary during the life of the loan

- when interest and capital instalments have to be paid

- the circumstances in which the lender can claim early repayment of the whole loan

- the purpose for which the loan may be used

- any conditions you have to satisfy before the loan will be available, eg survey reports on buildings

- what information you have to provide to the lender during the lifetime of the loan, eg management accounts.

Making the application

Knowing your business
If you are asking someone to finance your business you will have to persuade them that placing their money in your hands is a good investment. This means you must be able to:

- tell them what your business involves
- show them how their money will be used in your business
- convince them that the future of your business is secure and that you will have the resources to pay any interest due and eventually repay the capital sum advanced to you.

If you have been in business for some time already, you should be prepared to show a prospective lender your audited accounts. In addition the lender will want to see any management accounts and forecasts showing how you expect the business to perform in the future. Other documents of interest to a lender when considering your application will be:

- lists of current debtors
- lists of creditors
- VAT records
- current orders
- statements for any existing bank accounts
- details of existing loans, and any security and guarantees you have given relating to them, and your proposals for repaying them.

These will all help the lender form a picture of your business, its existing position and, most importantly, its ability to meet any loan repayments in the future should they advance monies to you.

Presenting a business plan
If you are starting a new business, you will need to present a **business plan** to any organisation from which you wish to borrow money. Not surprisingly, the lender will need a lot more detail if it is a new business than for an established business with a proven track record. On the other hand potential lenders will generally be prepared to offer help for people wishing to start up businesses. Before making an application enquire whether a business start-up information pack is available. They are free and often very useful. The lender may also have a specific format for business plans which it requires applicants to fill out.

Writing a business plan
There is no set format which all business plans should follow. However, there are a number of items which all business plans should contain. These are:

BUSINESS BUDGET

Month/Year | 1997–98

SUMMARY	ACTUAL	BUDGETED	OVER BUDGET	UNDER BUDGET	
Total income	54,050.00	44,780.00	9,270.00		
Total expenses	23,040.00	22,090.00	950.00		
Income less expenses:	31,010.00	22,690.00	8,320.00		

INCOME DETAILS	ACTUAL	BUDGETED	OVER BUDGET	UNDER BUDGET	NOTES
Sales	50,000.00	40,000.00	10,000.00		
Interest earned	100.00	200.00		– 100.00	
Fees	1,000.00	1,500.00		– 500.00	
Commissions	1,000.00	1,000.00			
Rent	1,500.00	1,500.00			
Royalties	200.00	300.00		– 100.00	
Other	250.00	280.00		– 30.00	
Total income:	54,050.00	44,780.00	9,270.00		

EXPENSE DETAILS	ACTUAL	BUDGETED	OVER BUDGET	UNDER BUDGET	NOTES
SELLING					
Salaries and wages	1,500.00	1,000.00	500.00		
Commissions	200.00	250.00		– 50.00	
Advertising	700.00	1,000.00		– 300.00	
Delivery	300.00	240.00	60.00		
Shipping	300.00	200.00	100.00		
Travel	500.00	300.00	200.00		
Other	200.00	300.00		– 100.00	
Total sales expenses:	3,700.00	3,290.00	410.00		
Percent of total:	16.06%	14.89%			
ADMINISTRATIVE					
Salaries and wages	300.00	400.00		–100.00	
Employee benefits	300.00	300.00			
Payroll taxes	1,400.00	1,400.00			
Insurance	580.00	580.00			
Loans	10,000.00	10,000.00			
Office supplies	190.00	200.00		– 10.00	
Travel & entertainment	240.00	300.00		– 60.00	
Postage	250.00	400.00		– 150.00	
Furnishings	150.00	150.00			
Contributions	170.00	180.00		– 10.00	
Dues	20.00	30.00		– 10.00	
Other	370.00	500.00		– 130.00	
Total admin. expenses	13,970.00	14,440.00		– 470.00	
Percent of total:	60.63%	65.37%			
SERVICE & EQUIPMENT					
Accounting	200.00	300.00		– 100.00	
Legal	300.00	500.00		– 200.00	
Utilities	1,500.00	1,200.00	300.00		
Telephone	400.00	260.00	140.00		
Equipment purchases	270.00	300.00		– 30.00	
Rent & maintenance	1,700.00	300.00	1,400.00		
Other	1,000.00	1,500.00		– 500.00	
Total S&E expenses:	5,370.00	4,360.00	˙1,010.00		
Percent of total:	23.31%	19.74%			

Fig. 9. A business budget. A new business will have no 'actual' figures.

- a description of the product or service which the business supplies

- a description of the market for the goods or services

- details of the people who manage the business and any key employees

- a brief schedule of the assets used in the business and whether they are owned outright, subject to any security, or held subject to any credit, lease or hire agreement

- a **budget** showing what the income and expenses of the business will be over the next year at least, including the interest and other sums payable in respect of your loan

- a cash flow statement which will detail any periods during which expenditure exceeds income and you may have to ask the lender for additional funds.

An example of a budget, which should form the foundation of a business proposal for use when applying to a bank, is set out in Figure 9.

Meeting the lender
Lenders make decisions based not only on the financial information presented to them, but also on the people who manage the business. When you meet with a lender it is important that you create the right impression. The best ideas sometimes fail to find the finance they need to grow into mature businesses because the proprietor/inventor does not inspire confidence as a businessperson. You must convince your lender that your business idea is sound and that you are capable of managing it in an effective manner. Some tips for meetings:

- always be punctual or advise of delay

- always go armed with more information than you think you will have to give to the lender

- take enough copies of documents which will be needed at the meeting

- never make any promises you know will be impossible to keep

- do not be afraid to tell the lender you need time to consider one of its suggestions or proposals thoroughly

- prior to the meeting ask if it would be helpful for the lender to bring other people who know about your business such as the auditors or solicitors.

USING BUSINESS ASSETS AS SECURITY FOR LOANS

Giving security over assets

A lender will often require a business customer to provide security for any loan it makes. The type of security taken by a lender will depend on the assets used in the business. What does creating security mean? If a lender has security over an asset, it may sell that asset if the loan is not repaid on time and use the proceeds of the sale to repay any sums due. There are a number of documents which lenders use to create security.

Creating a legal charge

A **legal charge** is a type of mortgage. It is used to give a lender security over land and buildings. If you lease premises from which to run your business, you will need to check that the lease does not prevent you from giving a legal charge over your interest in the lease. If the lease contains a clause which states no charge may be created, you must obtain the landlord's permission before giving your lender security over that lease. If you do not obtain the landlord's permission before giving the legal charge, you run the risk of the lease being forfeited by the landlord.

Creating a debenture

If you run your business through a company the lender may ask you to give it security in the form of a **debenture**. This is a special kind of security document which only companies may create. It contains charges over fixed assets used in your business, like land, plant and machinery, and floating charges over consumables used in the business, like stock in a shop. The important point to remember is that once a debenture (some lenders will refer to the document as a 'fixed and floating charge') has been given, the lender has security over all of the assets used in the business such as:

- land, whether leasehold (there is the same need to check the lease as discussed above) or freehold

- the debts due to the business
- the plant and machinery which is owned by the company (but not any leased or hired items)
- the stock
- the benefit of any orders
- the goodwill of the business.

The lender can only enforce the security by selling the assets or appointing a receiver if you default on repaying the loan, if you are subject to insolvency proceedings (see below) or if there is some other serious breach on your part of the loan agreement. Appointing a receiver involves taking the running of the business out of your hands and putting it under the control of a specialist insolvency practitioner.

Setting off
One form of security a bank always has available is the ability to set off sums it owes the business (credit balances on the business accounts) against sums the business owes it (monies due on overdraft or loan accounts where a demand has been made). This right is available to a bank whether or not a special set-off agreement is signed. Sometimes a lender will try to extend this right by asking for a special agreement which allows it to set off a sum it owes a third party (say a credit balance on your personal account) against monies due to it from the business, of which you are a director.

GUARANTEEING BUSINESS DEBTS

Understanding guarantees
There can be no greater cause of disputes than the failure by customers to fully appreciate the exact nature of the obligations being undertaken when signing a guarantee of a third party debt. Of course, some misunderstandings result from the failure by lenders to explain in clear language what rights they acquire against guarantors. This section explains the obligations you take on when you sign a guarantee in favour of a lender.

You need to understand some jargon, which is best explained through an example. Assume your business is run through a company of which you are a director. It has a loan or overdraft from ABC Bank of, say, £25,000. You have signed a guarantee of that loan or overdraft in favour of ABC Bank. The company is what is called the **principal debtor**. You are the **guarantor**.

Repaying the loan

If for any reason the principal debtor does not repay the loan or overdraft immediately upon the lender making a demand, the lender can make demand upon you as guarantor for the full amount due. The lender does not have to sue the principal debtor first, or even take steps to sell any assets over which it may have taken security. It bears repeating.

> **The lender can take steps to recover the full amount from you as guarantor immediately, once the principal debtor fails to meet the demand made upon it.**

Most guarantees will make you liable for the following:

- the amount lent to principal debtor
- the interest on the loan or overdraft (which may run at a higher rate once default occurs)
- any costs which the lender incurs in enforcing its security, or suing the principal debtor or you as guarantor.

Limiting a guarantee

It is possible for you to agree a limit to your liability under a guarantee. To continue the example from above, you could ask ABC Bank to limit your liability to a fixed sum of £10,000. If you intend to limit the amount you have to repay under a guarantee, remember to make it clear that you are liable only for '£10,000' whether that is capital, interest or costs.

Acquiring rights as a paying guarantor

If you pay off the principal debtor's loan you will acquire certain rights. You have transferred to you all the rights which the lender had against the principal debtor. You also acquire the right to a payment from any other co-guarantors of the same debt. So in the example, if you were just one of five co-guarantors of the debt the company owed to ABC Bank (for example, along with four other directors) and you paid off the whole debt of £25,000, you would be entitled to the following:

- the benefit of any security held by ABC Bank over the assets of the company

- a contribution of £5,000 from each of the other four co-guarantors so as to spread the burden of the liability equally between the five co-guarantors.

You acquire these rights only when you have paid off the lender; you are said to be subrogated to these rights.

USING PROFESSIONALS TO HELP YOU

Taking on too much
It is difficult to both start up a business and deal with all of the formalities required to obtain finance for that business. There are many organisations which will be able to offer you assistance in most of the matters discussed in this chapter.

Using accountants
Accountants are a valuable resource who will be able not only to offer audit services but also guidance in setting up financing and managing a business. They will be experienced in drawing up business plans and representing intending borrowers in meetings with banks and other lenders. If you are unsure about your ability to cope with the process of seeking a loan they will be able to offer assistance, although you will be charged a fee for the service they provide.

Using lawyers
If you are to create legal charges and debentures which give a lender security over land, you will probably need to engage a solicitor to help you with certain registration formalities. Solicitors will also be able to advise on the detail of the terms and conditions attaching to a loan.

Using business advisory services
There are many free business advisory services available. Some addresses appear in Useful Addresses. These organisations will be able to give you advice on special start-up schemes, which are subsidised by the government and may offer loans at discounted interest rates or without insisting on personal guarantees if you run the business through a company.

A number of the clearing banks have business advisory departments which offers guidance on setting up a business. Their objective is partly to generate new business for the organisation but they often produce useful guides which are free.

Dealing with business debt

It is easy for a business to run into financial difficulty. Often the hardest part of dealing with escalating debt is to continue communicating with the person to whom the money is owed. It is essential that you continue to keep your business lender informed of any developments in your business, whether good or bad. Chapter 9 contains some advice on escaping from the debt trap.

CASE STUDIES

Jeff becomes an entrepreneur

Jeff is nearing the end of his studies and wants to become a partner in a new firm along with some friends. Without a proven track record in business to show a bank or other financier, he decides to consult an accountant to prepare a business plan. He has a good track record with his own bank and is willing to invest some of his savings in the new business. His bank agrees to lend money based on his plan and the good track record of his personal accounts.

Patricia decides not to sign a guarantee

Patricia has been asked by her boyfriend to stand as a guarantor of a business loan he wants to obtain. She takes the advice of a solicitor to make sure she fully understands the commitment she would be making if she signs. Although the bank which has requested the guarantee is not asking her to create a second mortgage over her new home, she is told that if she could not meet a demand made under the guarantee and her boyfriend's business failed, she could still lose her home. The bank could apply for a charging order to enforce any judgement they obtained against her under the guarantee, in order to sell her home. After discussing the matter with her boyfriend, they both agree she should not become a guarantor.

John finds a new source of finance

John discusses the various ways in which he might improve the cash flow of his business with his branch manager. They decide that he should **factor** his business debts. The business receives 'advance payments' for sales, against the debts owed by customers of the business, to the special factoring company which is an associated company of his bank. John gets quicker access to funds from the monies due to the business and the factoring company takes a commission. The business will benefit from a better cash flow and so will have to draw less on the overdraft and loan facilities.

QUESTIONS AND ANSWERS

Q *My company has received a demand to repay a loan. How long have I got to pay this?*

A That depends on the terms of the loan agreement. For overdrafts you are usually obliged to repay immediately the demand is received. For business loans other than overdrafts a longer period may be specified in the agreement.

Q *As a director of a company or a partner in a firm am I personally liable for business loans?*

A Directors of companies are not personally liable to repay business loans. They may become liable for the loan if they guarantee it. Partners in a firm are generally automatically liable, along with all of their co-partners, for business loans made to their firm.

Q *Are business loans the only source of business finance?*

A No. There are venture capital companies which specialise in investing in new and emerging companies. They do so by buying shares in the company rather than making a loan to it on security of a debenture over the company's assets.

DISCUSSION POINTS

1. What is the best way to finance the purchase of new premises or equipment for a business?

2. Apart from the amount of the loan and its cost to your business, what are the important factors in choosing a lender?

3. How much interest can your business safely afford to pay on its business loans?

8
Troubleshooting

IDENTIFYING PROBLEMS

Deciding...fight or flight?

During the past twenty years I have had occasion to complain about the service I have received from my bank on just three occasions. The first two occasions were for pretty minor things. If I am honest in one case I was to blame. The last time was something which could have had serious consequences for me if I had not been lucky enough to spot the error early enough to put it right. On that occasion I made no complaint, I simply changed banks. The purpose of recounting this story is to point out that when things go wrong you need to look at what has happened with some objectivity. Ask yourself a few questions:

- Is the bank really in error? Have they done something entirely proper which you just do not happen to agree with or like?

- Have they broken their part of the bargain?

- Are you in a position to get the banking services you want from somebody else?

- Do you feel strongly enough about what has happened to spend some time and money putting it right?

- What do you want the bank or financial organisation to do to put this right?

Your ultimate sanction is to take your custom elsewhere, to move your accounts to another organisation. If you have outstanding loans or an overdraft, that means making arrangements to repay it and applying for new facilities. In my case, on the third occasion I thought my bank had made an error, I did not want to go to the trouble of giving the bank a second chance as I could easily move accounts. If you want to stay with the bank which you believe has made an error, you must balance the fact that you will have to continue your relationship with them against the desire to take all steps necessary to obtain a remedy for their failures.

Telling the bank there is a problem
It is very important that you tell your bank there is a problem as soon as it arises. There are two reasons for this:

- By keeping quiet and continuing to operate your account as normal, you may waive any remedy including the right to compensation.

- By alerting the bank as early as possible, you may make it easier for them to put matters right if they are in error.

There are cases, for example, where customers have noticed irregularities on their statements but not taken steps to alert the bank, where the matter was brought to the attention of the bank late they have been held not to be responsible for repaying sums wrongfully taken from such customers' accounts.

MAKING A COMPLAINT

Making the first move
Take the initiative. Do not wait for the bank to spot their error and put it right. If you are not happy with the actions (or inactions) of your bankers, you need to put your view to them firmly but fairly. Human nature is such that some mistakes will raise your blood pressure to the extent that you simply need to let off steam at some bank official. Remember that the person you speak to initially may not be the person responsible for making the mistake. He or she may, however, be the only person who can put matters right for you quickly and painlessly. Make your unhappiness felt but remember that banking is a business, not a school of perfection. Being firm is more effective than being abusive.

Writing a letter of complaint
The first thing you need to decide is to whom within the organisation your letter should be addressed. In most financial organisations this will be the branch manager. In credit card

12 Any Avenue, Anytown
Anycounty BB0 3BB

Mr Branch Manager
Mybank Limited
Any Street
Any Town AN1 3BC   Date

Dear Mr Manager

Re: Your Charges
My Current Account No. 110000444

I am writing to you to complain about the bank charges which have been deducted from my current account.

My complaint
The following charges have been deducted in the last month from the above account.

3.4.97 £15.00 unauthorised overdraft fee
5.4.97 £8.00 service fee
10.4.97 £12.00 cheque return fee.

I do not agree that those charges should have been deducted and have never authorised such a deduction.

My reason for complaining
On the 1st April 1997 I arranged a small overdraft facility of £100 to cover expected fluctuations on my current account. I had a conversation with Ms Smith, one of your Account Managers, who confirmed that the facility had been approved and that no fee would be payable for the facility. All of the above charged concern the use of this authorised overdraft facility which your bank told me would be made available at no cost.

Remedy
I would like you to confirm that the amounts deducted from my account will be recredited to it and that no further charges will be imposed in this respect. If you do not agree to remedy this situation I would ask you to let me have details of any complaints procedure operating at Mybank and the name of the person to whom I should write to pursue my claim.

Timescale
I expect to hear from you as soon as possible and in any event within the next ten days.

Yours sincerely

A. N. Other

Fig. 10. An example of a letter of complaint.

companies and hire purchase companies there will be either an account manager or customer services manager. If you are in any doubt, call the organisation and ask them who deals with customer complaints. It is important that your message reaches the people within the financial organisation whose task it is to resolve problems. They are the people who will know what to do with it and so be least likely to let it sit on their desks for a while until they figure out who to send it to.

Putting your case across
The following points need to be dealt with in your letter of complaint.

1. Setting out the facts
Set out concisely the circumstances which have given rise to the problem. There is no need to describe every conversation you have had with the organisation dealing with the matter. Put in enough information for a person coming to the matter new, but with the ability to see the bank's records, to understand what the problem is, where it arose within the organisation and who has been dealing with it to date.

2. Setting out your concerns
The letter should say why you are unhappy with the service you have received. Most importantly you must describe any monetary loss you may already have suffered, or may incur, or extra expense to which you have been put as a result of the problem having arisen. For example, if you have had to pay interest on a bill which you instructed the bank to pay but which the bank failed to action, this needs to be brought to their attention.

3. Setting out your request for remedial action
If you simply set out the problem, you leave it for the bank to suggest a solution. You run the risk that they will suggest something which you believe to be inappropriate. Always make it clear in the initial letter what action you believe the organisation should take to put the matter right. If you are seeking compensation, set out how you have calculated the amount you are asking them to pay. Should they be waiving interest due on sums you owe them to compensate you? If your letter indicates a way to solve a problem, the bank may be more inclined to act, rather than admit their fault and await some as yet unspecified claim or request for compensation.

4. Reserving your rights

If you are going to continue to use the services provided by the organisation against whom you are making a complaint, make it clear that by doing so you are not giving up any rights you may have in relation to their failures in the past.

Keeping records of a complaint

If you are in a dispute with any commercial organisation, it is sensible to keep a record of any conversations, meetings and letters which might be needed if the dispute is investigated by a third party such as a court. Here are a few tips:

- keep copies of the letters you send

- make a written note of telephone conversations and meetings as soon as possible after the event

- acknowledge receipt of letters promptly, especially if you are going to spend some time preparing a full response

- make sure the records you keep are truthful and accurate

- never put something in a record which you would not wish a third party to see – clever asides may not appear so clever to an impartial third party.

TAKING A COMPLAINT FURTHER

Climbing the chain of command

Most financial services organisations have complaints procedures which you should follow at least initially. If you do not obtain what you consider to be a proper response, you have to decide whether to continue your fight by informing someone else within the organisation or by trying to get a third party to intervene.

One of the most effective ways to stimulate action in a large organisation is to write to those at the very top of its management structure. The chairman or chief executive of a large bank or building society will have staff whose tasks are to see that letters to the head of the organisation are dealt with promptly and effectively. That is not to say you will get what you asked for, but you should at least obtain a response if that has become part of the problem!

Enlisting the help of the ombudsman
An ombudsman is an independent official who has the power to help resolve complaints and disputes. There is an ombudsman for both banks and building societies and one which deals with insurance. Contact details are given in Useful Addresses. Both schemes issue free guidance.

Dealing with the ombudsman
The procedure is, briefly, as follows:

• If you do not receive a satisfactory response to your complaint from the organisation against whom the complaint is made, you write to the ombudsman. The ombudsman will not consider your complaint until the organisation's internal complaints procedures are exhausted.

• If the ombudsman believes your complaint has merit and falls within his terms of reference, he will send you a formal application pack to complete so that he can take the matter up with the relevant organisation.

• The ombudsman decides who is at fault. If the bank or building society is at fault, they will be asked by him to settle your complaint, usually by paying compensation assessed by the ombudsman. If the ombudsman decides against you, he will write to you and explain his reasons.

• If there is still some disagreement, the ombudsman can direct the financial organisation to pay a sum up to £100,000.

• You always have the ability to reject the ombudsman's recommendations and pursue the matter in the courts.

Limits to the schemes
The ombudsman schemes are available to most small companies and individuals. Companies with a turnover in excess of £1 million cannot use the scheme. Nearly all of the bigger banks and building societies are members of the schemes. If you are in any way unsure whether you can use the scheme (or which scheme you should use – bank, building society or insurance), a telephone call to any of the ombudsman offices should resolve this problem. The schemes are free of any charge.

Accessing computer data
Many financial organisations will keep the vast majority of their records on computer. If you wish to obtain a copy of computer data about you, the Data Protection Registrar will be able to help you if such data is not provided to you upon request. Under the Data Protection Act 1984 organisations which keep personal data on computers are obliged to give copies of that data to the individual concerned if he or she makes a request in writing. The organisation may make a small charge (currently £10) for dealing with the request. You also have the right to have the data erased or corrected if it is wrong. If you suffer loss as a result of unauthorised use or any inaccuracy in relation to the data, you may be entitled to compensation. These rights can be helpful in many sorts of disputes, particularly those concerning credit references.

Details of the Data Protection Registrar are given in the Useful Addresses section at the end of the book.

USING THE SMALL CLAIMS PROCEDURES

Finding information
If the dispute with your bank, building society or other financial organisation involves less than £3,000 there is a relatively quick and simple way to get a court official to look into the matter. Attached to most County Courts is a Small Claims Court. You will find the details of your nearest County Court in the telephone directory and they will be able to tell you what procedures to follow.

Making a small claim
Your local Small Claims Court will give you the forms you need to complete in order to make a claim. You will have to be able to describe the claim concisely, and be prepared to tell the court official face-to-face what your claim is about and what you believe should be done about it. Once you have filed a claim, details will be sent to the organisation against whom the complaint is made, which will be asked for its response. A date for a meeting at the Court will be set so that both sides can put their case forward. The meeting is conducted in an informal manner without the usual complicated rules of evidence applied by County Courts and the High Court. The use of solicitors at such meetings is discouraged.

The Court will make a ruling which has all the force of a full County Court or High Court judgement. The procedure usually takes up to nine months, from filing the claim to receiving an adjudication.

OBTAINING PROFESSIONAL ADVICE

Instructing solicitors
Some disputes are incapable of being resolved through any means other than the County or High Courts. Although you are able to represent yourself before either of these courts, it is a task which you should only take on if you are willing to devote a lot of time to learning the procedures which have to be followed by litigants. You will also need the self confidence to be able to represent yourself before a judge and be able to argue against a barrister or solicitor representing the bank or building society. If this is too much for you to take on, you will need to think about instructing a solicitor to advise you on your claim and represent you in any court proceedings.

Finding a lawyer
If you do not already know a good lawyer, the best thing to do is to contact your local Citizens Advice Bureau or The Law Society. They will be able to recommend someone who will be able to help. Libraries also have directories which contain lists of solicitors' firms and the areas of law in which they specialise. Your local Legal Aid Office may also be able to help you.

Asking the right questions
Once you have found a solicitor you will need to ask the right questions if you are to make best use of their services. Here are some of the matters which you should take up straight away.

Paying for the solicitor's services
Make sure the basis upon which you have to pay the solicitor is agreed at the outset. Most solicitors charge by the hour, so you will need to ask for an update on the costs once a certain monetary limit has been reached. The solicitor will be able to advise you whether you will qualify for Legal Aid. Remember that if you get Legal Aid, you may still have to pay part of the costs out of any compensation you receive if you are successful in court. A solicitor will also be able to tell you whether the costs of a case are covered by any insurance you hold.

Obtaining an opinion on the merits
One of the first things you will want to know is the chances of your success should the matter go to court. Although no solicitor will guarantee you will win, they should be able to tell you at a fairly early

```
                                                    12 Any Avenue
                                                         Anytown
                                                       Anycounty
                                                        BB0 3BB

Your Solicitor
Messrs Firm & Co
Court House
Anytown
Anycounty BB1 3CC                            Date

Dear [Solicitor's name]

Re: Dispute with Mybank Limited
I am writing further to our conversation earlier today when you agreed to act for me
in a dispute which has arisen with Mybank.

The facts
The facts which give rise to the dispute concern a direct debit order which I
cancelled some time ago. Despite a clear written instruction to Mybank to make no
further payments pursuant to the direct debit authority signed in favour of Anytown
Insurance Co Limited, last year the bank has continued to pay sums under it.

I enclose the following:

1. A copy of the original direct debit form.
2. A copy of my letter to Mybank withdrawing the authority to make payments under
the direct debit.
3. Copies of notes of telephone conversations between me and Mr Manager at
Mybank.
4. A copy of Mybank's letter to me explaining they are not liable for any mistake.

Timescale
To date I have not received any assurance that the next direct debit will not be paid
on 7th July 1997. I would like you to obtain confirmation on my behalf from Mybank
that no further payments will be made, as soon as possible and in any event before
7th July next.

Objective
I wish to obtain compensation from Mybank for the monies wrongly paid out of my
account and a refund from Anytown Insurance Co. Limited. You have agreed to let
me have your opinion on the merits of my claim within the next ten days.

Costs
As agreed you will be paid on the basis of your firm's hourly charge out rates which
are £50 per hour and the costs will depend on the time spent on the matter. I have
authorised you to run up costs to a limit of £400 plus VAT. Before the costs rise any
further you will contact me for a further authority.

If you require any further information please let me know within the next seven days.

I look forward to hearing from you.

Yours sincerely,

A. N. Other
```

Fig. 11. An example of a letter of instruction to a solicitor.

stage whether or not you have a good chance of success. It is critical that you obtain an opinion on the merits of the case as soon as possible. This should enable you to judge whether to cut your losses and drop the case, or to plough more time and money into pursuing it. Remember that if you lose, you face a bill not only from your own solicitor but one from the winning side's legal team as well!

Agreeing a timetable
One of the commonest complaints levelled against the civil court system is the time it takes to deal with cases. The average case takes something between nine months to a year to come before a judge, depending on which area of the country you live in. Your solicitor will be able to give you a good idea of how long you will have to wait for your day in court.

Settling a claim
Most cases are settled before the first court hearing. It is often cheaper and quicker to settle out of court. Such a settlement also allows you to limit your exposure to costs, both your own and the other side's if you lose in court. At the outset you should discuss with your solicitor the parameters for any settlement so that he can negotiate on your behalf.

Supervising a solicitor
The quality of a solicitor's output is in some respects a reflection of the input from his client. It pays to monitor progress carefully and to make sure you are giving your adviser all the help you can.

Using other professionals
There are other types of professional organisations which may be able to help you in any dispute over financial services. Accountants can audit records if there is a disagreement over your bank statements or the conduct of your business accounts. They are also able to advise on financial difficulties, as discussed in Chapter 9.

There are also specialist companies which offer to check your statements and bank charges, interest and other costs to ensure that you are not being overcharged.

CASE STUDIES

Jeff complains to his bank manager
Jeff has cancelled a direct debit used to pay a subscription to his

PLAINTIFF MAKES CLAIM	TIME PERIOD	DEFENDANT HAS CLAIM MADE AGAINST IT
Plaintiff issues a writ	Any time before the limitation period expires, usually six years in cases where a debt is being pursued but two years if negligence is the issue	No action
Plaintiff serves the writ on defendant	Within one year of issuing the writ usually, although this period can be extended	No action
No action	Within 14 days of having the writ served upon him	Defendant must acknowledge service of the writ to avoid a judgement being entered against him
Must supply full particulars of claim before the defendant can be forced to answer	Within 14 days of receiving full particulars of the plaintiff's claim. This period is usually extended by the courts if cause is shown	Defendant must serve his defence to the claim made, particularly of which are contained in the writ or another document served later called the Statement of Claim
Directions for trial and disclosure of evidence which is to be presented at trial	Normally a few months after each side has finished giving the other details of its case	Directions for trial and disclosure of evidence which is to be presented at trial
The trial	Normally between nine months and two years after service of the writ by the plaintiff	The trial

Fig. 12. Approximate timetable for resolving a dispute in the courts.

local sports centre. On checking his bank statement, he finds that despite having cancelled the direct debit authority, £200 has been taken from his account. After telephoning the bank, he writes to the manager giving him a copy of the original letter cancelling the direct debit. The manager recredits Jeff's account immediately and reclaims the sums wrongly taken from the account under the indemnity given by the sports centre when it took the direct debit authority.

Patricia complains to the Banking Ombudsman

Patricia notices that several amounts have been taken from her account, apparently by use of her ATM card. When she checks her records she confirms that she had not used her card on those occasions. She writes to the bank, following their complaints procedure to the letter. The customer service department at Greenbank finally write to her stating that the bank's computer systems could not have made any error and that if she did not use the cash card as shown on the statement, someone else must have used it. Sheepishly her father tells her that the bank's computer systems are perfect.

Patricia decides to send a letter to the Banking Ombudsman with copies of all the relevant correspondence. She knows that it will take some time for him to deal with the complaint, but hopes he may have had similar cases. She has been told by her father that the bank would defend any claim she brings against it very strongly and she does not want to fight the claim on her own.

John instructs his solicitors

John has been told by his bank that they are freezing all of his business accounts to prevent him drawing any further sums on the various overdraft and loan facilities. The matter is so critical to his business that he immediately instructs his solicitors and his accountants to investigate the matter. They write to the bank asking why it has taken such action without any warning. The bank replies that it has the ability to make demand because the business has failed to pay sums due on the contractual repayment dates. John's solicitors obtain a ten-day grace period before the bank will take any further action and to give John some time to find further funds. He is expecting a big cheque shortly from a customer.

QUESTIONS AND ANSWERS

Q *How much will a solicitor or accountant charge?*

A Most solicitors and accountants charge at an hourly rate, so the bill depends on how long they spend on the case. If you are not offered a fixed fee for the job, you will need to agree one in advance of the work being done. You may be entitled to Legal Aid for some disputes.

Q *Is it better to settle a claim rather than go to court?*

A It is almost always better to settle a claim rather than go to court. Court proceedings are very expensive and you risk having to pay a part of the other side's costs if you lose.

Q *How long will it take to transfer my account to another organisation?*

A Most transfers can be completed within a few days. For businesses special arrangements can be made to ensure there is continuity of banking services during the transition.

DISCUSSION POINTS

1. How would you prefer to resolve a dispute with your bank: by letter, in a meeting or on the telephone?

2. What qualities would you look for in a professional adviser?

3. How much would you be prepared to pay in terms of time and money to resolve a dispute with your bank?

9
Escaping the Debt Trap

CONTROLLING DEBTS

In their booklet *Dealing With Your Debts*, the National Debtline
(see Useful Addresses) sets out a number of golden rules to be
followed by someone who has problems with escalating debts. The
first of these rules states:

> **'Don't ignore the problem: it won't go away and
> the longer you leave it, the worse it gets.'**

This chapter is to help you plan a strategy to cope with escalating
debt. You have to make two commitments as early as possible to
deal with the issues which debt raises. These are:

- to be able to justify the money you spend and any further debts
  you incur

- to recognise that the only way out of the debt trap is to alter
  something you are currently doing or not doing, whether that is
  spending too much, failing to talk to your creditors or not
  claiming benefits you are entitled to from the state.

ASKING FOR HELP

There are numerous people who will be able to give you guidance on
escaping the debt trap. The Useful Addresses section gives contact
details for several organisations who give free and confidential
advice. They can help you plan a strategy and give you advice on
how to deal with lenders and other creditors, including advice on
whether your lender can repossess your home.

PLANNING A STRATEGY FOR PAYING DEBTS

Communicating with creditors

If you are to come to some arrangement with your creditors it is essential that you keep in touch with them. One of the commonest causes of complaint from creditors is that the person who owed them money did not alert them to a problem. A creditor is more likely to take a sympathetic view of any proposals to settle his claim if he has been forewarned and kept up to date with any change in your financial position.

Getting help from creditors

Most organisations to which money is owed are well aware of the problems which debt can cause. Some creditors such as gas, electricity and telephone companies actually have special internal departments whose main task is to help customers in financial trouble (see Useful Addresses). Most creditors will realise that a more enlightened approach, working *with* the customer, will be in its own interests because this will produce a greater return than immediately running off to court to sue or bring bankruptcy proceedings. Creditors view court proceedings as a last resort because they are costly and time-consuming.

Being honest

The greatest danger for someone in financial difficulty is to create an atmosphere of suspicion amongst his or her creditors. The easiest way to create that atmosphere of suspicion is to disappear from the creditors' view by failing to respond to letters or answer telephone calls. Similarly it is essential not only to communicate with creditors but to ensure that the information given to them is accurate and up to date. This does not means that you must circulate creditors with a set of personal accounts every week but it does mean that their questions must be answered truthfully. As you will see below creditors do need to be circulated in a formal manner when certain proposals are put to them.

Offering a reasonable deal

If you are going to stand any chance at all of having your proposals accepted by creditors, you must be in a position to convince them that what you are offering is reasonable in all the circumstances. Good communication with them beforehand lays the foundation on which your proposal will be built.

Keeping records
It is useful to keep a written record of all enquiries you receive and when these have been answered. Keeping such a journal, and copies of letters, will enable you to show other creditors that you are going about the business of putting your financial house in order in a businesslike manner.

Dealing with people
It is human nature for some people to react badly when they receive bad news. There may be creditors who, at least initially, generate some heat when told of your financial difficulties. Nobody likes to be on the sharp end of such an exchange, but remember that you are fulfilling your responsibilities to your creditors by telling them of the problem and putting forward a proposal to deal with it. Do not be deflected from your objective of having your proposal accepted by heated words spoken in haste.

Planning a proposal

Treating all creditors fairly
The most important rule of any proposal which you put forward is that it must treat all creditors fairly. It must also leave you with

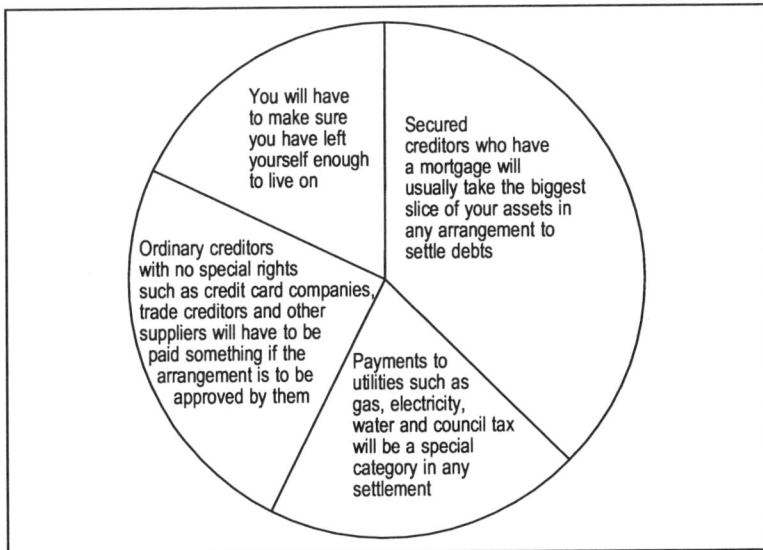

Fig. 13. A strategy for debt repayment.

sufficient funds to make a living in the future. Treating creditors fairly does not mean treating all creditors the same. The existing rights of creditors must be taken into account in deciding how they will be dealt with in the proposal. For example, it is no good putting forward a proposal that all creditors should be paid 70 per cent of their claims when your mortgagee knows that if it had to sell the property it could reclaim its debt in full. It would clearly not wish to participate in such a proposal.

> **Your debt repayment strategy must divide up your available assets fairly but leave you enough to live on whilst it is being implemented.**

Secured creditors
A secured creditor is one who holds a charge or mortgage over your house or some business asset. Such a creditor is entitled to sell the assets covered by the charge or mortgage and apply the proceeds of sale (after deducting the reasonable costs of sale) against payment of your debt.

Hire purchase and lease creditors
The owner of goods you have bought on hire purchase, conditional sale or lease rental is in a similar position. Such creditors may repossess the goods and after giving value for the goods claim only for the balance of the debt, if any. For example, if you have bought a television on hire purchase and the total payments under the agreement are £900, if the repossessed set has a secondhand value of £500 the claim against you will be £400. The agreement may allow the owner to claim certain costs such as the costs of collecting the television and other default payments, for example interest on the outstanding balance at a higher rate than normal.
    The point to bear in mind in any proposal is that the rights of creditors in this category to reclaim goods or sell assets must be acknowledged in any terms of settlement which are offered to them.

Ordinary creditors
Ordinary, or unsecured, creditors have only one right and that is to sue for the debt which is due to them. For example, your credit card company can only sue you to recover the debt. It cannot claim to repossess the goods you have bought with your credit card.
    Other unsecured creditors must all be dealt with in the same

manner unless there is some exceptional circumstance which demands that they be treated preferentially. Remember that you will possibly be called upon to explain to other unsecured creditors why you have conferred special treatment on somebody who at first sight appears to have no greater claims. It is important that you can justify your action. Failure to persuade the general body of unsecured creditors that one of their number deserves special treatment could wreck any chance of having your proposal accepted.

Utility companies
The providers of services such as gas, electricity and telephone companies will have the right not only to recover the debt by suing but also to stop providing those services. Special arrangements will obviously need to be included in any proposal to ensure that these services are continued. This will usually mean setting aside a sum of money to pay these service providers in full for future supplies.

Deciding how much to offer creditors
The object of any proposal is to settle creditors' claims by either:

- paying them a certain percentage of their claim which they accept as payment in full

or

- paying creditors in full but over a more extended period than was agreed at the outset.

In either case, from your point of view it is essential you are put in a position where you have enough money left to meet essential living expenses and are not constantly under pressure from creditors to make extra payments. The proposal should allow you to get on with the rest of your life, having provided your creditors with the best return they could reasonably expect given your financial problems.

Paying the right amount
The hardest decision you will face is the amount you agree to pay to your creditors. There is no sense in pitching this unrealistically high to convince creditors to accept; this would be a short-term solution achieved at the cost of further long-term problems. Be prepared to justify the amount calculated for reasonable living expenses. You must have the details of how you arrived at these figures and be prepared to show them to creditors who ask for them. What is

reasonable to one creditor will be an outlandish extravagance to a second and an unreasonable tightening of the belt to a third. The amount of money you set aside for yourself each month must be within a broad range that most people would accept as necessary.

Ask yourself whether there are changes in your lifestyle which it would be reasonable for third parties to expect you to make. Remember that the alternative to putting in place voluntary proposals may be bankruptcy, or at least court proceedings, and either can result in you being forced to change the way you live in order to meet your creditors' claims.

Setting out the terms of the proposal

There is no standard set of terms to include in a proposal to put before creditors, but certain matters should always be dealt with.

Amount of payments

The amount which any creditor is to receive must be clearly set out. If you are asking a creditor to accept less than the full amount in final settlement of his claim, that must be stated with absolute clarity.

Timing of payments

Most creditors will be seeking weekly or monthly payments as this will spread their risk. They will not be eager to accept a larger sum paid annually as the risk of default is greater. Monthly or weekly payments allow a creditor to monitor your performance in keeping to the terms of the proposal more closely.

Interest payments

Some creditors, such as those claiming under credit agreements, mortgagees, banks and trade creditors, will probably have agreements with you which provide for them to receive interest on outstanding monies. Your proposal must specify whether interest will continue to be paid on the sum due to the creditor and, if so, at what rate. Remember that some creditors increase the level of interest if the payment terms in the original agreement are not adhered to. You should try to ensure that no interest at so-called 'default rates' is charged. One option is to offer each creditor the same rate of interest, the justification for this being that it treats all creditors equally. Any interest which accrues on debts must be capable of being serviced, ie paid each month. Creditors will view a failure to service interest as the first sign that you are unable to perform the agreement set out in your proposal.

Creditors' rights
If a creditor agrees to your proposal, they should be happy to accept that they will not enforce any rights against you (such as repossessing goods) which they might have had at the time the proposal was put in place, provided you keep to the terms set out in your proposal. Normally you would state in the proposal that a creditor could only exercise such 'original rights' if you default under the new proposal.

IMPLEMENTING ARRANGEMENTS WITH CREDITORS

Making informal arrangements
An informal arrangement is one in which you seek the agreement of your creditors without going through any special procedures laid down by law. You are simply making contractual arrangements with all of your creditors which will bind both them and you according to their terms. You can go about obtaining those agreements in whatever manner you think will be most effective. Typically this will involve:

- making an initial approach to inform the creditor of your position
- putting detailed proposals to all of your creditors
- meeting with your creditors or discussing the proposals with them
- revising the proposals to meet any points made by creditors
- sending out a final version of the proposals to each creditor
- obtaining final agreement from each creditor.

Gaining creditor approval
As each creditor accepts your proposals, the agreement between you and that particular creditor will become effective. Some creditors may make it a condition of their agreement becoming effective that you obtain all other creditors' agreements in due course or over some specified period. In that case the package of proposals only replaces the original relationship when the condition has been satisfied.

There are no special rules laid down which you must follow. However, it is possible to choose to follow a special but more formal procedure, which is to be found in the Insolvency Act 1986.

Making formal arrangements

Individual voluntary arrangements
Part I of the Insolvency Act 1986 introduced what are known as
individual voluntary arrangements. Special procedures must be
followed and consequently your freedom of action in gaining your
creditors' agreement is more limited. In particular, in order to put a
proposal for an individual voluntary arrangement to creditors you
will need to employ an **insolvency practitioner**.

Consulting an insolvency practitioner
An insolvency practitioner will usually be an accountant. Any local
firm of accountants, solicitors or Citizens Advice Bureau will be
able to point you in the right direction. You will also find in the
Useful Addresses section some telephone numbers where you can
obtain help in finding an insolvency practitioner in your locality.

An insolvency practitioner will charge a fee for taking on the job,
although the size of it will depend on the complexity of your case.
For an average individual voluntary arrangement the fee will be
around £400. It is important that you clarify the fee at the first
meeting with the insolvency practitioner.

After finding out what assets and liabilities you have, the
insolvency practitioner will produce a standard form set of
proposals to be put to creditors.

Putting a proposal to creditors
The proposal is sent to all creditors along with a notice convening a
meeting at which they will vote whether to accept or reject the
proposals. If more than 75 per cent accept the proposals they
become binding on all creditors who received them, even if they
voted against them. Once accepted, the original claim of the
creditor is replaced by his claim to a payment in accordance with the
voluntary arrangement drafted by the insolvency practitioner.

The benefit of this scheme is that, if one creditor is being difficult,
it can be used to force him to settle his claim on terms which all
other creditors have found acceptable. The disadvantages are the
additional costs of involving an insolvency practitioner and the fact
that all creditors, no matter how big or small, must be involved in
the process which can make the arrangement cumbersome. Another
disadvantage is that the failure to obtain acceptance of the
proposals at the creditors' meeting will normally mean that
bankruptcy proceedings are the only available option.

UNDERSTANDING BANKRUPTCY AND LIQUIDATION

Being made bankrupt

If an individual is unable to pay debts as they fall due and is unable or unwilling to enter into an arrangement, he or she may be made bankrupt. A trustee, who will be a qualified insolvency practitioner, will be appointed to deal with all of the assets with a view to selling these to pay off debts. The money collected by the trustee is shared equally between all creditors. Once all assets have been sold and the money distributed to creditors, the bankruptcy will be ended and the debtor is left to start again with a clean slate.

Consequences of bankruptcy

Being a bankrupt has a number of consequences in addition to taking the management and control of your assets out of your hands. It will disqualify you from holding certain offices, such as directorships or becoming a local councillor.

Understanding liquidation

When a company becomes insolvent, it may be put into liquidation. A liquidation may be voluntary in the sense shareholders of the company decide the company cannot continue and vote to have it wound up. There is another process which is known as compulsory liquidation. In this case a creditor of the company presents a petition to the court asking it to wind up the company because it has refused or is unable to pay its debts.

In either case a liquidator, who is a qualified insolvency practitioner, is appointed by a meeting of the creditors of the company to sort out the company's affairs. He will sell the company's assets and out of the proceeds of sale will pay some or all of a creditor's claims.

Once all of the assets have been sold and the money distributed amongst creditors, the company's life is terminated by being struck off the Register of Companies.

Directors of liquidated companies

A liquidation has certain consequences for the directors of the company. The liquidator must report upon their conduct which, if found to be dishonest or unreasonable, can result in proceedings being brought against them. These proceedings may result in the directors being disqualified from acting as directors or managers of any other businesses for a set period which can be as long as fifteen years.

Bankruptcy	Voluntary Liquidation	Compulsory Liquidation
You file a petition.	You call a shareholders meeting.	A creditor files a petition.
A court hearing is held which may be attended by your creditors. You will be made bankrupt and a trustee in bankruptcy appointed to look after your assets.	A resolution is passed to wind up the company and a liquidator appointed. A date is set for a creditors meeting.	A date for a court hearing is set. You have the right to contest the petition.
After all your assets have been sold your creditors will be paid a dividend. The bankruptcy order is then discharged.	At the creditors meeting the creditors have the right to vote in their representative as liquidator to sell the assets of the company for them.	At the hearing the court may make a winding up order, in which case a liquidator is appointed to sell the assets of the company and to hold a creditors meeting in due course.
Once the bankruptcy order has been discharged you are free to take control over your assets again.	Once the liquidator has sold all the assets of the company it is struck off the register at Companies House.	Once the creditors meeting has been held the liquidator sells the assets. When he has done this the company is struck off the register.

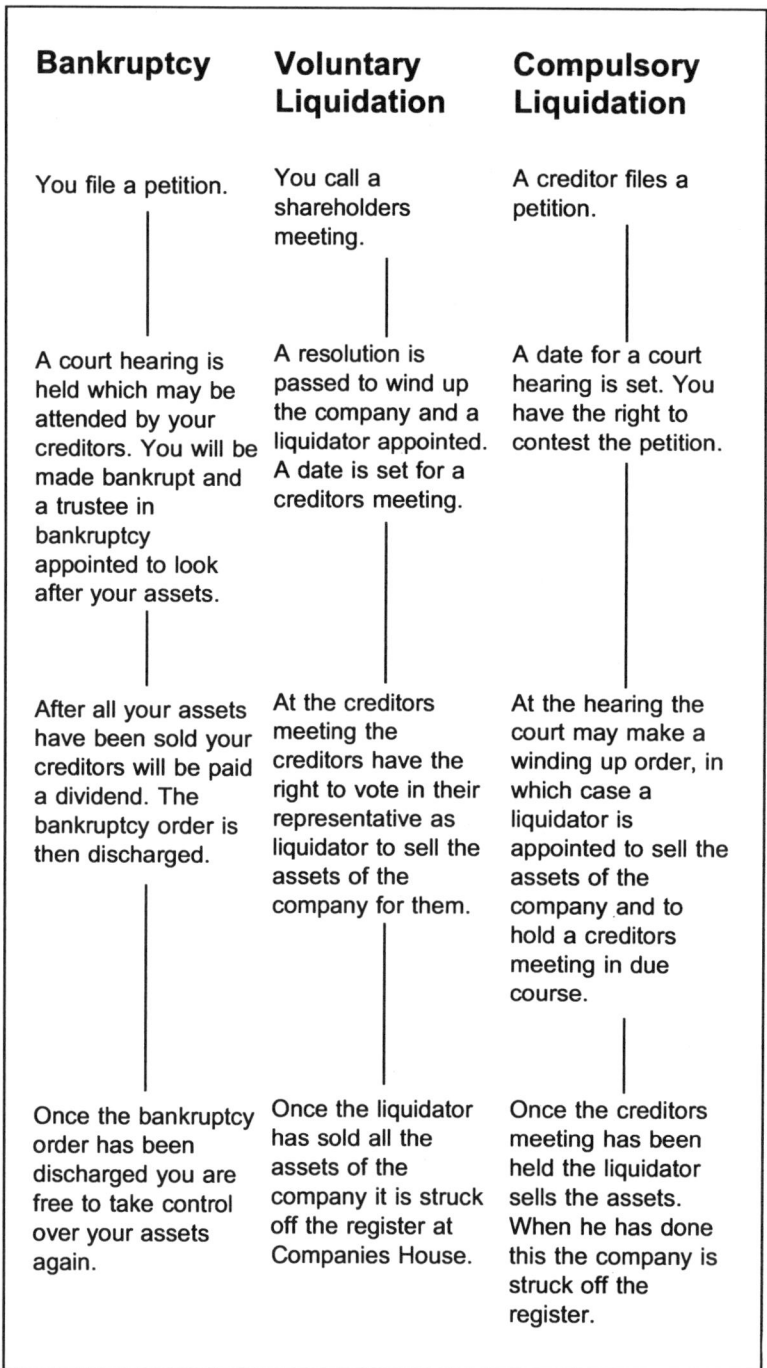

Fig. 14. What happens in a bankruptcy and the liquidation of a company.

Normally neither the personal assets of directors or shareholders in a company can be used by a liquidator to meet the claims of the company's creditors. Only if the director allowed the company to continue trading when he knew it was insolvent will his personal assets be at risk.

CASE STUDIES

Jeff closes his business

Jeff has decided that being an entrepreneur is not for him. The partnership he set up has not gone well and is in danger of failing. He decides to see his ten major creditors to ask them to accept 80 per cent of the claims in full and final settlement of their debts. The other creditors will be paid in full as they are all very small claims. He writes to each with proposals making it clear that the only reason for paying other creditors in full is the number and small amount of their claims. The ten major creditors are not happy but see that the only alternative is to make the partnership bankrupt, in which case they may get nothing. They appreciate that Jeff has obtained funds from his family to make the scheme viable and that they would not be liable for the debts without Jeff having obtained their cooperation.

Patricia asks for extra time

Patricia has managed to run up a significant credit card debt with several companies. She telephones one of the free debt advisory services whose telephone number she found in the telephone directory, *Yellow Pages* or *Thompsons Local*. Following a free discussion with a counsellor she writes to each of the credit card issuers, asking for extra time to pay and giving details of her income and outgoings. They agree but ask for slightly higher monthly payments once she is in a position to repay the debt in six months. She is asked to return her cards or destroy them to make sure the debt does not escalate further.

John faces liquidation

John's business has failed and the bank has demanded repayment of his business and personal loans. John decides to call in an insolvency practitioner to put his company into liquidation to avoid further losses to trade creditors. He also asks another insolvency practitioner to prepare an individual voluntary arrangement for him so that he can clear all of his personal debts in an organised manner.

QUESTIONS AND ANSWERS

Q *To which creditors should I give priority in making payments?*

A You will need to continue to pay debts to gas, electricity and other suppliers who may cut off essential services whilst you develop your plan to deal with all creditors. In the initial stages of sorting out a plan you will also need to take steps to ensure your mortgagee does not repossess your property and this may involve making payments to it.

Q *Should I speak to creditors before obtaining some advice?*

A No. Try to obtain advice first as this will help you to organise which creditors you speak to first and what you say to them. If in the meantime creditors contact you, it is essential that you are open and honest with them. You may find it necessary to tell them that you are seeking advice and will be in touch with them later. You must obtain your advice as quickly as possible to avoid upsetting your creditors. If they do not think you will deal with their debt they will take steps to recover their money.

Q *Does the fact that I have been bankrupt stop me from earning a living?*

A No. Once a bankruptcy order is discharged you are free of any restrictions on what you may do with your assets. Even whilst a bankruptcy order is in force, you will be encouraged to continue to earn an income although your trustee in bankruptcy may have control over how your income is used.

DISCUSSION POINTS

1. What categories of creditors do you have to deal with in your proposal?

2. Do you know whether you are entitled to additional benefits to supplement your current income?

3. How could you reduce your current outgoings?

Glossary

Annuity. A sum of money paid to you each year of your life, often in monthly instalments, and which is bought from an annuity provider by paying it a lump sum the amount of which depends on the annuity rate.

Annuity rate. The ratio of the amount of lump sum payable to acquire a specified amount of annuity, eg paying £100,000 to obtain £9,000 per annum gives an annuity rate of 9 per cent.

Asset. Property which you can turn into money whether in the long- or short-term.

APR or **annual percentage rate**. The actual interest you will pay over one year, taking into account any periodic adding of interest to capital by the lender.

ATM or **automatic teller machine**. More commonly known as cash machines.

BACS or **bankers automated clearing system**. The commonest method for transferring funds electronically, for example when paying wages.

Bank giro credit. The most common form of paying money into a bank account or making a transfer of funds from one account to another.

Base rate. The rate of interest set by the Bank of England and used by lenders as a benchmark when setting the interest rates payable on loans.

Bond. Usually a form of investment account which pays a fixed or variable interest rate, but can also refer to issues of debt by companies on a recognised stock exchange.

Budget. An estimate of income and outgoings, usually completed for a period of a least one month but can be for a whole year.

Business plan. A summary detailing the expected performance of your business, usually for a period in excess of one year but no longer than five years, which will also detail its expected financial position.

Cash flow. The differences in your cash requirements from time to time throughout a year, also referred to as 'peaks and troughs' in cash requirements.

Charge. When used in the context of an account can be anything from an arrangement fee to a monthly fee, or a default fee for unauthorised overdrafts, but see also mortgage.

Charge card. A card which is issued to you and allows you to pay for goods and services up to a pre-set spending limit but which should be paid off in full each month.

Cheque guarantee card. A card issued by a financial organisation to its account holders which allows them to guarantee to third parties, such as sellers of goods, that a cheque under a certain limit (which may be anything from £50 to £250) will be met upon presentation for payment irrespective of the level of funds in the account.

Clearing cheques. The period of time it takes for a cheque to be credited to the payee's account and debited to the drawer's account.

Client agreement. Agreement which should specify the basis on which you are to receive advice on financial services and products and which should tell you whether your adviser is independent.

Consumer Credit Act 1974. A law enacted to protect people who enter into credit agreements of all types, including personal loans, credit cards and HP agreements but not debit cards and business loans.

Contribution rights. Rights which one guarantor obtains against any co-guarantors once he has paid more than his fair share of the guaranteed debt.

Credit. A credit to your account is a receipt of money into the account but credit also means taking on a borrowing of some sort whether through buying goods with a credit card or hire purchase agreement.

Credit card. A card which allows you to pay for goods and services up to a pre-set credit limit and which you do not have to pay in full each month.

Credit transfer. The transfer of funds out of one account (the transferor) and into another (the transferee).

Current account. An account which pays a lower rate of interest than a deposit account, but which carries with it a cheque book and certain other facilities which may not be available on a deposit account.

Debenture. A special form of charge used by lenders to obtain security over business assets of companies.

Debit. A debit entry is made on your account whenever you present a cheque or withdraw money from your account in some way.

Debit card. A card which you may use for goods and services without incurring any credit where the amount involved is debited to your account almost immediately after you use the card.

Defendant. The person against whom a claim is made in court.

Deposit account. A higher interest account than a current account which may restrict access to your money and may not offer cheque books and other services which go with a current account.

Direct debit. Authorising a third party to take sums from your account on a regular basis against its promise to make a refund in cases of error.

Disposable income. How much money you have left over each month after paying your monthly expenses and which you can use to invest.

Drawer. The drawer of a cheque is the person on whose account the cheque is written.

EFTPOS or electronic funds transfer at the point of sale. The system which allows you to pay for items by using a Switch, Delta or similar card rather than writing a cheque.

Endowment insurance. An insurance policy which pays a specified sum plus bonuses at maturity and which is often used in conjunction with a mortgage.

Equity. Used in relation to property subject to a mortgage, it is the difference between the value of the house and the amount of any loans secured upon it by way of a mortgage or charge.

Factor. A financial organisation which buys debts due to a business for a lump sum slightly less than the sum owed, but is paid the full amount of the debt when it is actually collected, so making a profit (factoring debts can improve cash flow in a business).

Financial profile. A statement showing your assets and liabilities and how much disposable income you have in any year.

Gross of tax. A payment usually of interest made without deducting lower or higher rate income tax. Usually given along with the rate net of tax for the purposes of comparison.

Guarantee. Any obligation you undertake which could result in you having to pay another person's debt to a third party (sometimes referred to as being a surety).

Guarantor. The person who gives a guarantee to a third party. There may be more than one guarantor of the same debt in which case they are said to be co-guarantors.

Illiquid assets. Assets such as your house which would take some time to be turned into cash.

Insolvency practitioner. An accountant or lawyer who specialises in bankruptcy and company liquidation.

Liability. Sums which you owe to other parties.

Liquid assets. Assets such as shares in a company or unit trust which can be sold quickly to give you a cash amount.

Loan agreement. The terms and conditions which stipulate what you have to pay to a lender and when you have to pay it.

Long-term assets. Property you intend to hold on to for a considerable period of time (usually more than one year) and which cannot be turned into cash quickly.

Mandate. Form of authority given to a bank or building society which allows them to follow instructions given on accounts, provided the authorised signatories specified on the form have signed.

Moneygram. A simple method of transferring cash from one place to another without using a bank account, for example through Western Union.

Money transfer. Any method by which funds are transferred from one account to another.

Mortgage. A form of charge which you give to a lender as security for your borrowing and which entitles it to sell the asset charged if you default on the loan.

National Savings. The savings and current account provider which operates through the post office network and which offers many tax-free financial products.

Net assets. The value of your total assets minus your total liabilities if the figure you arrive at is positive.

Net liabilities. The value of your total assets minus your total liabilities if the figure you arrive at is negative.

Net of tax. Usually refers to interest earned being paid after deducting basic rate tax, leaving you to pay any further tax if you are a higher rate tax payer or reclaim tax if you are not a taxpayer.

Notice of cancellation. A notice which is sent to people who enter into credit agreements governed by the CCA 1974 allowing them to reconsider and cancel the agreement within a specified time.

Ombudsman. An independent official who will investigate cases of complaint against service providers.

Overdraft. A loan account which is repayable on demand and which is used to fund temporary cash shortages.

Payee. The person to whom a cheque is made out.

Petition. Document presented to a court to start the process of making an individual bankrupt or a company compulsorily wound up.

Personal Equity Plan or **PEP.** A form of tax-free investment in shares or unit trusts.

Personal pension plan. A fully transferable pension investment into which you can pay contributions and on which contributions you will receive tax relief.

PIN or **personal identification number.** Issued with ATM and some credit cards.

Plaintiff. The person bringing a claim in court.

Principal debtor. The borrower whose debt to his lender you have guaranteed.

Realisable assets. Property you own which can be sold by you.

Savings account. An account which pays interest at a higher rate than a current account but which may not provide you with immediate access to funds or a cheque book.

Security. A charge or mortgage given by a borrower to his or her lender and which allows a lender to sell the property charged or mortgaged if there is a default on the loan repayment.

Smartcard. A form of electronic money which is encoded onto a plastic card which contains a microprocessor.

Standing order. An instruction by you to your bank to make a regular payment to a third party.

Term loan. A loan for any period longer than one year but not including overdraft facilities.

TESSA or **Tax Exempt Special Savings Account.** Allows interest to be paid free of tax.

Unit trusts. A share of a bigger fund, usually held by an insurance company or other fund manger, which consists of a wide range of investments such as shares, land and bonds.

Voluntary arrangement. A form of compromise under which creditors agree to accept late payment or a reduced payment in full settlement of their debts.

With-profits insurance. A form of investing monthly or annual sums, called premiums, with an insurance company which will pay a lump sum on the date the policy matures (falls due for payment) and which usually pays annual and final or terminal bonuses instead of interest.

Useful Addresses

BANKING GENERALLY

The British Bankers Association, Pinners Hall, 105–108 Old Broad Street, London EC2N 1EX. Tel: (0171) 216 8800.

The Building Societies Association, 3 Savile Row, London W1X 1AF. Tel: (0171) 437 0655.

The Chartered Institute of Bankers, Emmanuel House, 4–9 Burgate Lane, Canterbury, Kent CT1 2XJ. Tel: (01227) 762600. Also at 90 Bishopsgate, London EC2N 4AS. Tel: (0171) 444 7115.

The Consumer Credit Trade Association, Tennyson House, 159/163 Great Portland Street, London W1N 5FD. Tel: (0171) 636 7564.

The Consumer Credit Association of the United Kingdom, Queens House, Queens Road, Chester CH1 3BQ. Tel: (01244) 312044.

The Finance and Leasing Association, 18 Upper Grosvenor Street, London W1X 9PB. Tel: (0171) 491 2783.

Western Union. Tel: (0800) 833833.

DATA PROTECTION

The Data Protection Registrar, Wycliffe House, Water Lane, Wilmslow, Cheshire SK9 5AF. Tel: (01625) 545745.

HELP WITH DEBTS

The Council of Mortgage Lenders, 3 Savile Row, London W1X 1AF. Tel: (0171) 437 0655.

The Housing Corporation, 149 Tottenham Court Road, London W1P 0BN. Tel: (0171) 393 2000.

National Debtline, Money Advice Services, Birmingham Settlement, 318 Summer Lane, Birmingham B19 3RL. Tel: (0121) 359 8501.

Business Debtline. Tel: (0121) 359 7333.

Shelter, 88 Old Street, London EC1V 9HU. Tel: (0171) 505 2000.

INSURANCE

Association of British Insurers, 51 Gresham Street, London EC2V 7HQ. Tel: (0171) 600 3333.
British Insurance and Investment Brokers Association, 14 Bevis Marks, London EC3A 7NT. Tel: (0171) 623 9043.
Life Insurance Association, Citadel House, Station Approach, Chorleywood, Rickmansworth, Hertfordshire WD3 5PF. Tel: (01923) 285333.

INVESTOR PROTECTION

Investment Management Regulatory Organisation, Broadwalk House, 6 Appold Street, London EC2A 2AA. Tel: (0171) 379 0444.
Securities and Futures Association, Cottons Centre, Cottons Lane, London SE1 2RB. Tel: (0171) 378 9000.
Securities and Investment Board, Gavrelle House, 2–14 Bunhill Row, London EC1Y 8RA. Tel: (0171) 638 1240.

OMBUDSMAN

The Banking Ombudsman, 70 Gray's Inn Road, London WC1X 8NB. Tel: (0171) 404 9944.
The Building Societies Ombudsman, Millbank Tower, Millbank, London SW1P 4XS. Tel: (0171) 931 0044.
The Insurance Ombudsman, City Gate 1, 135 Park Street, London SE1 9EA. Tel: (0171) 928 7600.
The Personal Investment Authority Ombudsman, 3rd Floor, Centre Point, 103 New Oxford Street, London WC1A 1QH. Tel: (0171) 538 8860.

PROFESSIONAL ADVISERS

Institute of Chartered Accountants in England and Wales, PO Box 433, Chartered Accountants' Hall, Moorgate Place, London EC2P 2BJ. Tel: (0171) 920 8100.
The Law Society, 113 Chancery Lane, London WC2A 1PL. Tel: (0171) 242 1222.

STUDENTS

Student Loans Company Ltd, 100 Bothwell Street, Glasgow G2 7JD. Tel: (0800) 405010.

UTILITIES

OFGAS, Stockley House, 130 Wilton Road, London SW1V 1LQ. Tel: (0171) 828 0898. (Gas)
OFTEL, 50 Ludgate Hill, London EC4M 7JJ. Tel: (0171) 634 8888. (Telephone)
OFFER, 83/85 Hagley Road, Edgbaston, Birmingham B16 8QG. Tel: (0121) 456 2100. (Electricity)

Further Reading

Bankruptcy, National Debtline (1995).

Business of Banking, Don Wright and Wally Valentine (Northcote House, 1992).

Dealing with Your Debts, National Debtline (1995).

The Daily Telegraph Guide to Lump Sum Investment, Liz Walkington (Kogan Page, 1996).

Good Retirement Guide, Rosemary Brown (Kogan Page, 1996).

Guide to the Consumer Credit Act 1974, Professor Roy Goode (Butterworths, 1994).

Investing in Stocks & Shares, Dr John White (How To Books, 1997).

Investment Made Easy, Jim Slater (Orion Books, 1994).

Law of Domestic Banking, G. Penn, A. Shea and A. Arora (Sweet & Maxwell, 1987).

Lloyds Bank Small Business Guide, Sara Williams (Penguin Books, 1996).

Managing Budgets & Cash Flows, Peter Taylor (How To Books, 1996).

Managing Your Personal Finances, John Claxton (How To Books, 1996).

Money Lenders and their Customers, Karen Rowlingson (Policy Studies Institute, 1994).

Negative Equity – What Can I Do?, National Debtline (1995).

Which? Way to Save and Invest, The Consumer Association (1994).

Index

MANAGING YOUR PERSONAL FINANCES
How to achieve financial security and survive the shrinking welfare state

John Claxton

Life for most people has become increasingly beset by financial worries, and meanwhile the once-dependable prop of state help is shrinking. Today's financial world is a veritable jungle full of predators after your money. This book will help you to check your financial health and prepare a strategy towards creating your own welfare state and financial independence. Find out in simple language with many examples and case studies how to avoid debt, how to finance your home, how to prepare for possible incapacity or redundancy and how to finance your retirement, including care in old age. Discover how to acquire new financial skills, increase your income, reduce outgoings, and prepare to survive in a more self-reliant world. John Claxton is a chartered management accountant and chartered secretary; he teaches personal money management in adult education.

160pp. illus. 1 85703 328 0.

HOW TO START A BUSINESS FROM HOME
A practical step-by-step guide for beginners

Graham Jones

Most people have dreamed of starting their own business from home at some time or other, but how do you begin? The third edition of this popular book contains a wealth of ideas, projects, tips, facts, checklists and quick-reference information for everyone – whether in between jobs, taking early retirement, or students and others with time to invest. Packed with information on everything from choosing a good business idea and starting up to advertising, book-keeping and dealing with professionals, this book is basic reading for every budding entrepreneur. 'Full of ideas and advice.' *The Daily Mirror*. 'This book is essential – full of practical advice.' *Home Run*. Graham Jones BSc(Hons) is an editor, journalist and lecturer specialising in practical business subjects.

176pp. illus. 1 85703 126 1. 3rd edition.

COPING WITH SELF ASSESSMENT
How to complete your tax return and minimise your tax bill

John Whiteley

The Inland Revenue is sending out a colossal nine million tax returns in 1997 for the new self assessment system. The new forms and the new system of self assessing and paying tax represent a radical departure from the previous way of doing things. This book explains step-by-step how the new system works, how to fill in the new tax return, and what are some of the pitfalls to avoid. There are new powers for automatic penalties, surcharges and interest, and a chapter is devoted to avoiding these. The book also includes a chapter on how to pay less tax. Worked examples and illustrations are included throughout. Don't do your own self assessment before reading this book. John Whiteley FCA is a Chartered Accountant in practice. He has long experience of advising taxpayers in every walk of life. He lives near Exeter in Devon. His daily work involves dealing with the sort of people who would find this book most helpful, (the self-employed, retired people, etc.).

160pp. illus. 1 85703 394 9.

HOW TO UNDERSTAND FINANCE AT WORK
A guide to better management and decision-making

Peter Marshall

Are you in the dark about financial decisions? Are colleagues at work mismanaging the money side of things? Would you like a bigger say in financial issues? In plain English this new book demystifies the whole business of 'finance' and how to use it in any public or private sector organisation. With helpful examples and case studies, it explains how financial resources are best managed in practice, whether for capital or current projects. Use it to sharpen up your understanding, and help make the right financial choices in your own organisation. Peter Marshall BSc(Econ) BA MBIM is a Fellow of the Society of Business Teachers, and experienced educator in business subjects. He is also author of *Mastering Book-Keeping* in this series.

150pp. illus. 1 85703 086 9.

ARRANGING INSURANCE
How to manage policies and claims for everyday personal and business purposes

Terry Hallett

Most of us regard insurance as a necessary evil, and never bother to read our insurance policies, although we sign the contract documents and hand over our money. Only when a claim arises do we examine what we have bought. This new How To book provides a step-by-step guide explaining in simple easy-to-follow terms what to do when a mishap is suffered in the home, and how to pursue a successful insurance claim. It is written by an expert with 38 years' experience in the field of insurance claims handling. Terry Hallett FCILA ACCII MIM worked for many years as a Chartered Loss Adjuster for an international company. He was manager of a branch office for 25 years, and later an Associate Director of his company. He has also served as President of his local Insurance Institute.

176pp. illus. 1 85703 317 5.

MAKING A COMPLAINT
How to put your case successfully and win redress

Helen Shay

Whether you've bought faulty shoes or been sold an unsuitable investment; been over-charged by a bank or suffered the holiday from hell; this book guides you through the maze of complaints procedures, courts, ombudsmen and other forms of consumer redress. It makes the law user-friendly and shows you how to obtain compensation – fast. It shows the way to cut through the aggravation and achieve the best solution for you. Helen Shay is a solicitor of twelve years' standing. She has worked both in private practice and as an in-house lawyer for a major high street retailer – so has experience of consumer disputes from both sides. Currently with an ombudsman's office, she is well-versed in current consumer issues and the problems which can confront the individual versus large organisations. She also tutors and lectures part-time in commercial law, and is knowledgeable in contract, consumer credit, banking law, conveyancing and other legal areas affecting everyday life.

160pp. illus. 1 85703 102 4.

How To Books

How To Books provide practical help on a large range of topics. They are available through all good bookshops or can be ordered direct from the distributors. Just tick the titles you want and complete the form on the following page.

___ Apply to an Industrial Tribunal (£7.99)
___ Applying for a Job (£8.99)
___ Applying for a United States Visa (£15.99)
___ Backpacking Round Europe (£8.99)
___ Be a Freelance Journalist (£8.99)
___ Be a Freelance Secretary (£8.99)
___ Become a Freelance Sales Agent (£9.99)
___ Become an Au Pair (£8.99)
___ Becoming a Father (£8.99)
___ Buy & Run a Shop (£8.99)
___ Buy & Run a Small Hotel (£8.99)
___ Buying a Personal Computer (£9.99)
___ Career Networking (£8.99)
___ Career Planning for Women (£8.99)
___ Cash from your Computer (£9.99)
___ Choosing a Nursing Home (£9.99)
___ Choosing a Package Holiday (£8.99)
___ Claim State Benefits (£9.99)
___ Collecting a Debt (£9.99)
___ Communicate at Work (£7.99)
___ Conduct Staff Appraisals (£7.99)
___ Conducting Effective Interviews (£8.99)
___ Coping with Self Assessment (£9.99)
___ Copyright & Law for Writers (£8.99)
___ Counsel People at Work (£7.99)
___ Creating a Twist in the Tale (£8.99)
___ Creative Writing (£9.99)
___ Critical Thinking for Students (£8.99)
___ Dealing with a Death in the Family (£9.99)
___ Do Voluntary Work Abroad (£8.99)
___ Do Your Own Advertising (£8.99)
___ Do Your Own PR (£8.99)
___ Doing Business Abroad (£10.99)
___ Doing Business on the Internet (£12.99)
___ Emigrate (£9.99)
___ Employ & Manage Staff (£8.99)
___ Find Temporary Work Abroad (£8.99)
___ Finding a Job in Canada (£9.99)
___ Finding a Job in Computers (£8.99)
___ Finding a Job in New Zealand (£9.99)
___ Finding a Job with a Future (£8.99)
___ Finding Work Overseas (£9.99)
___ Freelance DJ-ing (£8.99)
___ Freelance Teaching & Tutoring (£9.99)
___ Get a Job Abroad (£10.99)
___ Get a Job in America (£9.99)
___ Get a Job in Australia (£9.99)
___ Get a Job in Europe (£9.99)
___ Get a Job in France (£9.99)
___ Get a Job in Travel & Tourism (£8.99)
___ Get into Radio (£8.99)
___ Getting into Films & Television (£10.99)

___ Getting That Job (£8.99)
___ Getting your First Job (£8.99)
___ Going to University (£8.99)
___ Helping your Child to Read (£8.99)
___ How to Study & Learn (£8.99)
___ Investing in People (£9.99)
___ Investing in Stocks & Shares (£9.99)
___ Keep Business Accounts (£7.99)
___ Know Your Rights at Work (£8.99)
___ Live & Work in America (£9.99)
___ Live & Work in Australia (£12.99)
___ Live & Work in Germany (£9.99)
___ Live & Work in Greece (£9.99)
___ Live & Work in Italy (£8.99)
___ Live & Work in New Zealand (£9.99)
___ Live & Work in Portugal (£9.99)
___ Live & Work in the Gulf (£9.99)
___ Living & Working in Britain (£8.99)
___ Living & Working in China (£9.99)
___ Living & Working in Hong Kong (£10.99)
___ Living & Working in Israel (£10.99)
___ Living & Working in Saudi Arabia (£12.99)
___ Living & Working in the Netherlands (£9.99)
___ Making a Complaint (£8.99)
___ Making a Wedding Speech (£8.99)
___ Manage a Sales Team (£8.99)
___ Manage an Office (£8.99)
___ Manage Computers at Work (£8.99)
___ Manage People at Work (£8.99)
___ Manage Your Career (£8.99)
___ Managing Budgets & Cash Flows (£9.99)
___ Managing Meetings (£8.99)
___ Managing Your Personal Finances (£8.99)
___ Managing Yourself (£8.99)
___ Market Yourself (£8.99)
___ Master Book-Keeping (£8.99)
___ Mastering Business English (£8.99)
___ Master GCSE Accounts (£8.99)
___ Master Public Speaking (£8.99)
___ Migrating to Canada (£12.99)
___ Obtaining Visas & Work Permits (£9.99)
___ Organising Effective Training (£9.99)
___ Pass Exams Without Anxiety (£7.99)
___ Passing That Interview (£8.99)
___ Plan a Wedding (£7.99)
___ Planning Your Gap Year (£8.99)
___ Prepare a Business Plan (£8.99)
___ Publish a Book (£9.99)
___ Publish a Newsletter (£9.99)
___ Raise Funds & Sponsorship (£7.99)
___ Rent & Buy Property in France (£9.99)
___ Rent & Buy Property in Italy (£9.99)

How To Books

___ Research Methods (£8.99)
___ Retire Abroad (£8.99)
___ Return to Work (£7.99)
___ Run a Voluntary Group (£8.99)
___ Setting up Home in Florida (£9.99)
___ Spending a Year Abroad (£8.99)
___ Start a Business from Home (£7.99)
___ Start a New Career (£6.99)
___ Starting to Manage (£8.99)
___ Starting to Write (£8.99)
___ Start Word Processing (£8.99)
___ Start Your Own Business (£8.99)
___ Study Abroad (£8.99)
___ Study & Live in Britain (£7.99)
___ Studying at University (£8.99)
___ Studying for a Degree (£8.99)
___ Successful Grandparenting (£8.99)
___ Successful Mail Order Marketing (£9.99)
___ Successful Single Parenting (£8.99)
___ Survive Divorce (£8.99)
___ Surviving Redundancy (£8.99)
___ Taking in Students (£8.99)
___ Taking on Staff (£8.99)
___ Taking Your A-Levels (£8.99)
___ Teach Abroad (£8.99)
___ Teach Adults (£8.99)
___ Teaching Someone to Drive (£8.99)
___ Travel Round the World (£8.99)
___ Understand Finance at Work (£8.99)
___ Use a Library (£7.99)

___ Use the Internet (£9.99)
___ Winning Consumer Competitions (£8.99)
___ Winning Presentations (£8.99)
___ Work from Home (£8.99)
___ Work in an Office (£7.99)
___ Work in Retail (£8.99)
___ Work with Dogs (£8.99)
___ Working Abroad (£14.99)
___ Working as a Holiday Rep (£9.99)
___ Working in Japan (£10.99)
___ Working in Photography (£8.99)
___ Working in the Gulf (£10.99)
___ Working in Hotels & Catering (£9.99)
___ Working on Contract Worldwide (£9.99)
___ Working on Cruise Ships (£9.99)
___ Write a Press Release (£9.99)
___ Write a Report (£8.99)
___ Write an Assignment (£8.99)
___ Write & Sell Computer Software (£9.99)
___ Write for Publication (£8.99)
___ Write for Television (£8.99)
___ Writing a CV that Works (£8.99)
___ Writing a Non Fiction Book (£9.99)
___ Writing an Essay (£8.99)
___ Writing & Publishing Poetry (£9.99)
___ Writing & Selling a Novel (£8.99)
___ Writing Business Letters (£8.99)
___ Writing Reviews (£9.99)
___ Writing Your Dissertation (£8.99)

To: Plymbridge Distributors Ltd, Plymbridge House, Estover Road, Plymouth PL6 7PZ. Customer Services Tel: (01752) 202301. Fax: (01752) 202331.

Please send me copies of the titles I have indicated. Please add postage & packing (UK £1, Europe including Eire, £2, World £3 airmail).

☐ I enclose cheque/PO payable to Plymbridge Distributors Ltd for £ [   ]

☐ Please charge to my ☐ MasterCard, ☐ Visa, ☐ AMEX card.

Account No. [ ][ ][ ][ ][ ][ ][ ][ ][ ][ ][ ][ ][ ][ ]

Card Expiry Date [ ][ ] 19   ☎ Credit Card orders may be faxed or phoned.

Customer Name (CAPITALS) ....

Address ....

.... Postcode ....

Telephone .... Signature ....

Every effort will be made to despatch your copy as soon as possible but to avoid possible disappointment please allow up to 21 days for despatch time (42 days if overseas). Prices and availability are subject to change without notice.

[Code BPA]